SARDI'S

The Story of
a Famous Restaurant

Mr. and Mrs. Vincent Sardi, Sr.

SARDI'S

THE STORY OF
A FAMOUS RESTAURANT

BY

VINCENT SARDI, Sr.

AND

RICHARD GEHMAN

HENRY HOLT AND COMPANY
NEW YORK

This book is dedicated by Vincent Sardi
to his wife, Eugenia Pallera Sardi

Acknowledgments

Thanks are due all those people who assisted Mr. Sardi in recalling stories about his restaurant, notably Virginia Perry, Eva Condon, Ward Morehouse, Guthrie McClintic, Louis Schonceit, Renee Carroll, Jimmy Malinsky, John Brasi, Felix Appino, Alfred Drake, Leonard Lyons, Harry Hershfield, Michael Sloane, Bert McCord, Irving Hoffman, Lawrence Langner, Roy Roberts, Irving Mansfield, Sid White, Gary Stevens, Jules Ziegler, William Liebling, Mrs. Louise Beck, R. Nelson Hickman, Helen Keller, John Golden, Giovanni Robotti, Oscar Kanny, and the others who so generously aided by verification or contribution. Particular thanks must go to Garrison Sherwood, of the New York Public Library, a man with an encyclopedic knowledge of the stage since 1900, for his patient willingness to run down obscure facts; to George Frank, for his assistance in collecting some of the recipes; and to Everett De Baun, for help during interviews and in digging out odd bits of information. I also wish to thank D. R. Feigley, Jr., Robert Fraunfelter, and Julia Lindelow for their cooperation. Finally, a debt is owed to Mr. Sardi's wife, Eugenia; his son, Vincent, Jr., and his daughter, Anna, for continuing aid throughout the project.

R. G.

Contents

SARDI'S

The Story of
a Famous Restaurant

Meet Vincent Sardi

A RESTAURANT that serves first-class food prepared in a kitchen of character, serves it courteously and swiftly in attractive surroundings, at prices which are not out of reach or reason, and has been doing all this over a good long period of time—such a restaurant may with justification be called a great one. Sardi's, at 234 West 44th Street in New York City, just west of Broadway in one of the most active blocks of the entire theatrical section, is great by these standards, but its fame does not rest primarily on them. Sardi's is famous because it is unique in the United States and, for that matter, in the world. Sardi's is *the* restaurant of the American theater, so much so that many people consider it a part of the theater. To call into service an overworked simile, Sardi's is to theatrical people today what the Mermaid Tavern is said to have been to Shakespeare and his companions. Its regular customers are actors and actresses, producers and directors, writers and press agents, composers and choreographers, set designers and lighting engineers and creators of costumes, stagehands and electricians—anybody who is anybody in mummery, and a goodly parcel of nobodies, too. As the Elizabethans are said to have conceived and written and cast out of the Mermaid, so, for more than three decades, twentieth-century thespians have availed themselves of Sardi's. The

[1]

uses to which they have put it are virtually endless; the restaurant has been described not only as a place for eating,
drinking, and socializing, but also as a message center
and news headquarters, lovers' rendezvous, production and
financing office, audition studio, casting center, and, on in-
numerable occasions, psychiatrist's couch. Even seasoned ob-
servers, wise in the mores of Broadway, are perennially
astonished by Sardi's continuing popularity. One night in
1952, after a look-in, the veteran critic Ward Morehouse
wrote that "the informal Sardi show, given by the people of
the theater without knowing they're performing at all (is
still) one of the most extraordinary in this hemisphere." No
one would dispute this claim. A man standing in Sardi's for
a year during the after-theater supper hour could easily com-
pile a fairly exhaustive index to the contemporary stage
simply by writing down the names of people waiting for
tables or standing at the small bar.

There are varying theories as to how Sardi's came to be so
closely identified with the theater. One holds its convenient
location to have been responsible; but, after all, there are
more than a hundred restaurants in the theatrical district.
Another maintains that it is because actors love to run in
packs; this overlooks their well-known ability to suddenly
develop new enthusiasms. If mere herd-instinct were the reason, other places nearby, discovered by leaders of certain
cliques, would certainly be as heavily patronized, or more so.
Actually, the secret of Sardi's success, and the key to its fame,
lies in the personality of its owner.

In a piece to the memory of the late Dinty Moore written
last December, the columnist Ed Sullivan included Vincent
Sardi's name in a list of great Broadway hosts who had passed
on. Reminded that Mr. Sardi was still quite demonstrably
alive, Sullivan exclaimed, "Why, I'll be damned—somehow,
I'd thought the old gentleman'd been dead for years." Thus,
in a somewhat roundabout way, Sullivan was paying tribute
to Vincent Sardi's legendary stature. This legend has been

established and carried on by the customers, whose loyalty is something close to fanaticism. A list of these patrons would include nationally known personalities like Robert Montgomery (who in earlier, harder times used to check his hat on credit when he ate in Sardi's), and by lesser-known, actors' actors such as Roy Roberts (who plays supporting roles on the stage and screen). The best way to introduce Mr. Sardi, and to show what he has meant to his customers over the years is to let Roberts tell it in his own words, as he did one night in the restaurant while reminiscing. He was speaking of his first meeting with the proprietor.

"I was a kid," he said, "in New York for the first time, looking for the breaks. I had been in carnivals before that, tent shows, broken-down stock companies, everything but Tom shows and the Healey and Bigelow medicine outfits. I came to New York and somebody told me Sardi's was the place where the actors went, and the producers, the directors —everybody. That, I thought, is for me. So I come in and I sit down, and the next thing I know I am doing it big. I am buying drinks for everybody I meet, making the impression, and all I have is about $15. The check comes, and if I am not mistaken it is for seventeen or eighteen. I asked to see the owner. He came up. 'Yes, yes, what is it?' he asked. I explained to him that the bill wanted more money than I had. I babbled it out as fast as I could. I told him I would leave him my watch and my ring, and come in before noon the next day with the money for the check. He drew himself up— that great, dignified face, the grand manner, you know—and he said, slowly, 'You have no money?'

" 'That's right, sir,' I said, 'but I'll—'

" 'Actor?' he asked.

" 'That's right.'

" 'Just new here?'

" 'Yes, sir.'

" 'Why've you come to Broadway? To be seen, is that it? To get a part?'

" 'Yes, sir.'

"He smiled. He took the check and put it in his pocket. He said, 'I think you'll pay when you get a part.' "

At this point Roberts paused for breath, an expression of awe crossing his face. "It was like—well, nothing like that ever happened to me. And then, to make it even more unbelievable, as I was going out, he was standing at the door. He put out his hand to shake mine. He said, 'I'm glad to know you. Please come and see us often.' *In his hand was a $20 bill!*"

A book nearly the size of this one could be filled with similar confessions from beneficiaries. Some of the stories might be flavored a little, some slightly expanded—what actor can resist fattening his own part?—but all would be rooted in fact and in devotion.

Now, it should be understood that Mr. Sardi did not become the object of Broadway's esteem because he is a soft touch. This certainly must have been one reason some actors made his place their second home, but if it had been the main reason he would not have as many friends today as he does, since prodigal moneylenders usually wind up lonely. He attained, and held, his distinction almost in spite of his open-handed nature, and because of his cheerful, philosophical disposition, his quick sense of humor, his appreciation for the temperaments of his customers (and for temperamental differences), his awareness of their struggles, his ability to encourage them when they needed it, and perhaps for his ability to gently knock them down a bit when they needed that. There is no telling how many people he helped along by sending them to see, or introducing them to, other people he knew; there are so many stories of this kind told by grateful performers that they tend to become monotonous. Also, there is no telling how many careers he must have influenced indirectly, so to speak, by slipping the names of his favorites quietly into conversations with powerful writers, producers,

and directors. His strategy was always perfect: he never mentioned his own enthusiasm at first. He would inquire, as one
professional to another, how so-and-so's performance had
been. He would listen with interest to the reply, and finally he
would state, with dignity, his own prejudice—a highly effec-
tive performance, one for which scores of talented people are
thankful today.

Before he retired five years ago, Mr. Sardi was usually at
the front for lunch, dinner, and supper, greeting all guests
as they came, most of them by name. He was affable, polite,
and attentive, but anything but servile. An old acquaintance
has said that his innate dignity was apparent in his smallest
gesture. "Nobody who ever really knew Dad ever called him
anything but 'Mr. Sardi,'" his son, Vincent, Jr., has said.
"If anybody came in and demanded to see 'Vincent,' it was
almost a cinch that he wanted to cash a bum check." In
appearance, Mr. Sardi is commanding. He seems taller than
his medium height because he is a husky man—he weighs
around one hundred eighty—and because he carries himself
with a military erectness, more probably a hang-over from
his days as a waiter in the fine London hotels than from his
service in the army in Italy. He is a handsome man with a
strong nose, a high forehead, and a leonine mane of white
hair; it is not hard to imagine his having been a hand with
the ladies before he met his wife. (Unlike many marriages of
the theater, this one has endured—has endured, in fact, for
forty-two years!) The gravity of his customary expression is
frequently punctuated by a warm, spreading smile, accompanied by a low chuckle. His clothes are cut in the London manner and they are faultless; most of his suits, some of which he
has had for nearly twenty years, are subdued grays and browns
of some hard-surfaced fabric. A handkerchief is always
folded neatly in his breast pocket. Although he owns nearly
two hundred neckties, he most often wears a navy blue bow
with white polka dots. He has never worn anything but bows,
just as for years he has never put his feet into anything but

shoes manufactured by a certain Dr. Keller, whom he discovered soon after he came to the United States. He likes to mention that Dr. Keller made shoes for Abraham Lincoln. Remembering a time in London when he spent his last shilling on shoes which a flash rainstorm melted off his feet, he began buying pair after pair of Dr. Keller's. Even today some of them lie wrapped in their original boxes in his clothes closet, to the acute despair of his wife.

Mr. Sardi's meticulousness in dress runs through his entire personality and underscores his relationships with everyone he knows. He is meticulously sensitive about the feelings of others, to a degree, in fact, that is almost Victorian. The reader who is looking for scandalous accounts of high life along Broadway will not find them in the pages following. Books of this kind generally contain some references to drinking matches; there is nothing of the kind in here, except one affectionate reference to a young man who died before his time. Mr. Sardi knew carousers and topers by the score, but although he was never a total abstainer himself, he always kept aloof from the heavy drinkers and their parties. An acquaintance who saw him often during the thirties remembers that when one of his regular customers began drinking excessively, the sight seemed almost too much for him; he would hastily shrug into his overcoat, turn the restaurant over to his head waiter, and go for a walk around the block. During Prohibition he deliberately kept himself from earning a modest fortune. Although friends kept urging him to sell liquor, and although most of his regular customers flocked across town to Tony's, he never turned his place into a speak-easy. There was no question in his mind as to what he should do: he loved the country, so he abided by the country's law. There was also another reason.

He has said, "Even if I had been tempted to break the law, as so many others were doing, there were the children to think about. I thought, 'Suppose I get arrested? What will Vincent and Anna think if they see the black police wagon pulling up to the door, and the cops taking their father away? They will see that picture as long as they live."

But as usual, he did not allow his standards for himself to influence his opinion of another. One of the best friends he and his wife had was Texas Guinan, who in 1927, when her 300 Club was knocked off, claimed it as her forty-seventh pinch.

This does not mean that he did not occasionally rebuke a customer. More than one actor can remember an instance in which Mr. Sardi gave him hell for appearing in the place without a shave or in an unpressed suit. "How will you look to a producer?" he would demand. "How do you expect to get a part looking like that? Look—here is a dollar. Get a haircut. Get a shave. Press your suit. Come in smiling; look like something!" Occasionally his rebukes took a humorous turn. When the New York *Times* was building the annex that now runs the building from 43rd to 44th Streets, and places the rear right next door to Sardi's, the excavations and constructions made a good deal of noise. Consequently, Mr. Sardi kept most of the tables along the east wall vacant. One day Turner Catledge, managing editor of the paper, brought to lunch Mrs. Arthur Hays Sulzberger, wife of the publisher. Mr. Sardi greeted them cordially and seated them at an east-wall table. Seconds later they were startled by a thunderous explosion. The wall shook; the silverware clattered on their table. Catledge glanced at Mr. Sardi, who was scrutinizing a reservation list. "Shall we move?" he asked Mrs. Sulzberger. "No," she said, firmly, "it serves us right. We'll stay here." As they went out, Mr. Sardi inclined his head, as usual. Catledge, looking at him sharply, thought he saw him wink.

Mr. Sardi's strict respect for the law, noted above, is not only a part of his naturally scrupulous, tidy nature; it also has to do with his patriotism, which is as deeply felt as his religion. His love for his adopted country, is genuine without being a flag-waving, Yankee-Doodle-Dandy exhibitionism. He became a citizen in 1921, and his wife automatically became one with him. The days of his marriage and the births of his son and daughter aside, it was the happiest day of his life. He set about earnestly to become an American in every way. A detective friend told him he ought to join a lodge; he joined a lodge. Some friends from Italy belonged to Italian-American societies engaged in Rotarian projects of municipal improvement; he dutifully became a member and even on occasion an officer. He was always, when he could afford it (and sometimes when he could not) a contributor to public and charitable causes; a couple of times he learned that he had been taken by con men, but even these instances did not deter him from contributing the next time. During the war there was no more active member of the home-front corps. In addition to his work with the Stage Door Canteen, which will be set down later in this book, he kept up a correspondence with more than a hundred of his customers who were in the service. Some of them he knew only slightly. In conversation he is lucid, imaginative, and resourceful, but it is an effort for him to write in English; yet every night after he had closed the place he would sit down and deliver himself of three or four letters to his boys. He still has many of the letters he received in return. He still talks of the time that Alfred Smith, an actor, wrote him of finding a Sardi match cover in the mud of a Chinese jungle. He speaks with relish of how Jimmy Cannon, now the sports columnist of the New York *Post,* during the war a GI combat correspondent, wrote him on the personal stationary of Adolf Hitler.

Whenever a serviceman came home on pass or furlough, he did not have to look for free entertainment at the Stage Door Canteen, which, incidentally, was next door to the restaurant. The boy could be certain that Mr. Sardi would feed him and pick up the tab—and perhaps even introduce him to one of the fresh young faces of the wartime theater. As anyone might gather from all this, Mr. Sardi was an avid war bond salesman and buyer. After shaking hands with a customer who had just dined in his place, he would invariably say, "Now, don't forget—buy a bond!" Evidently feeling that such efforts and his own purchases were not enough, he made contributions of the interest on the bonds he had bought for himself and his family. In 1945 the Secretary of the Treasury reported in a press release that he had contributed nearly $6,000 in interest and other cash offerings. People who read about it in the papers congratulated him. He seemed embarrassed; after all, in his view, it was only a fulfillment of part of his duty. Continually conscious of his duty, he is also perpetually and vocally grateful for what the country has done for him. The pages he wrote in longhand as preliminary material for his autobiography are interrupted almost tediously by devout expressions of thanks. He will undoubtedly be mildly irritated—although he will never express it—when he discovers that many of these paeans have been excised.

Mr. Sardi has known nothing but hard work since boyhood. Now that he is retired the pattern has been altered somewhat, but it has hardly been broken. In truth he is retired only officially; he still goes to his restaurant at least five days a week, except in the summers, and he is still as interested in the business as he was when he was in sole control. In the mornings he comes in around ten-thirty, often bringing with him provisions he has bought at some farmer's stand out on Long Island, or perhaps some fish he and friends took at Southold the day before. After turning these over to the steward he goes into a brief consultation with his old friend John Brasi, the manager, who came to work for him in 1927, after he had moved from his first site, down the street where the St. James Theatre is now located, into the present building. Then he retires to his office and goes over bills, peers into checkbooks, reads through his correspondence. He still writes a great many letters to friends overseas, and nearly every day he gets a letter from some customer from whom he has not heard for years. The latter are generally sponstaneous expressions of thanks for his kindness and hospitality from customers long since forgotten—but always, when he has searched his memory for a moment, he can hook the signature to a face. Then he sets about writing a polite and grateful reply. While he is at this, his son, Vincent, Jr., comes in, ready to go downstairs to take his place at the front door. They exchange a few words, and the young man leaves. Many fathers who have passed on a going business to a son would attempt to maintain some measure of control in retirement; Mr. Sardi is as respectful to his boy as though he himself were an employee. When he offers advice, he does it much as he might have recommended the *canelloni* to a customer in his days on the floor.

Upon finishing his round of chores for the day, Mr. Sardi frequently goes downstairs to the kitchen, orders a sandwich or something light, and eats it at a table in a station the waiters use as their own dining section after the customers have cleared out. Then, if it is a pleasant afternoon, he takes a stroll about town, or more rarely, goes downstairs to see if there is some old friend, such as Harry Hershfield, Lou Schonceit, or John Golden among the late luncheon trade. Many afternoons he goes to visit sick friends. His loyalty is anachronistic in these times, and his word is firm. Some time ago, when he and his wife were dining with friends, it was suggested that they all take a short vacation within several months. Mr. Sardi and his wife agreed. As time went on, it became evident that it would be inconvenient for him to go at that time. Yet, because the friends were looking forward to the trip, he would never have considered suggesting a postponement. "I told them we would go, so we will go," he said to an acquaintance. "I don't want to go, but what can I do?"

Throughout most of 1952, Mr. Sardi occupied many of his mornings and some of his evenings in the preparation of material for this book. When the idea was first suggested to him, he was dubious. "I do not think I know enough for a book," he said. "I am not sure that people would be interested." In three or four two-hour morning sessions, he quickly

ran over the high spots of his life. "Well," he said, "I do not
know what more I can say." Then one question would lead
to a story, and that to another, and soon he would be talking
steadily, and always chronologically. During the early weeks
of the collaboration, he would write out pages in long hand,
long yellow pages of lined tablet paper, covered with a light,
slanting, penciled script, with many of the words spelled
phonetically. These he would present the next morning,
always with a weary sigh, and always with some deprecatory
remark, such as, "Well, I don't know if this will be any good
or not." Time and again he despaired; he could not see how
anybody would be interested in what he had to say. A writer
for a national magazine came in to do a short article; when
it appeared, several of Mr. Sardi's friends were upset. The
reporter had not bothered to check some facts and had
phrased certain material in a way that offended the subjects.
Mr. Sardi was ready, then and there, to abandon his memoirs.
It was only when he was reassured that he would have absolute control over the final copy that he was persuaded to go
on. When he was questioned on the facts he had written on
the tablet paper, and asked to elaborate and expand, his interest revived somewhat. As the days wore on, the memories
began to act upon each other in the manner of a chain re-
action. No sooner was one chapter completed than it had to
be altered to admit another anecdote. Old friends cooperated
enthusiastically in stimulating his memory, and more addi-
tions were required. The task of collaborator gradually split
up and settled into those of transcriber, rearranger, and
editor.

But none of this explains Mr. Sardi as a pivotal figure in
the Broadway scene. It does not show why his place so completely captured the fancy of theatrical people, practically
from the day of its opening. Part of this explanation may lie
in his understanding of the loneliness of creative individuals
(he has some remarks to make on this later on). Or it may
be that he, having been deprived of a family himself in boy-

hood, was determined to create one for himself and his customers. Everybody who has gone to Sardi's over a long period
of time inevitably begins every conversation about the place
with a reference to the family atmosphere that exists there.

But there is another, perhaps more important part of the
explanation. It lies in the fact that Mr. Sardi is something of
a theatrical figure himself. Few people love the stage more;
he and his wife go regularly to the theater and the opera
many times each month. When he speaks of his relatives, it is
his brother Domenico, the actor, now deceased, who receives
the greatest part of his attention. When he recalls his boyhood in Italy, he lingers over the incident of his appearing
in a play and therefore flunking an examination. There is
no question but that the theater has dominated his life, and
perhaps there is no denying his secret desire to have been an
actor himself. When he tells a story, the illuminations and
expressions in his face carry it along, lending emphasis and
color. One day when Dede Pritzlaff, a photographer, visited
him in his office to shoot some preliminary studies of him
and his wife, he jokingly dropped to one knee besides Mrs.
Sardi's chair, gazed at her adoringly, took her hand, smiled
broadly, and asked, "How about one like this?" His daughter
Anna says affectionately, "Dad is one of the hammiest people
in the world." Whether or not he still nourishes a desire to
perform, he certainly turned this urge to his own advantage and to that of literally thousands of others. Perhaps no
one else alive on Broadway today has done so much and
brought so much happiness to the people of the theater as
Vincent Sardi. Here is his book.

R.G.

"I Wish I'd Kept a Diary"

ONE OF THE SADDEST DAYS OF MY LIFE, if not *the* saddest, was the day I retired officially from the restaurant business. I had been looking forward to retirement, and so had Jenny, my wife, and I knew that Sardi's would be in excellent hands because my son Cino, who was taking it over, had been well trained. My wife and I had practically lived in the restaurant from the very first day when we had opened it in its old location a few doors to the west, and now we were looking forward to having plenty of time to ourselves. We hoped to travel around and see a good deal of this wonderful country, and we knew we would not find retirement boring; as I said to Lucy Freeman, the New York *Times* reporter who came to interview me, "We are very good friends, my wife and I." But as I went out the front door of Sardi's that last day and stepped into 44th Street, the fact of my retirement seemed to come to me for the first time. The street had been my home and headquarters for many years. It was 1947, and Jenny and I had been operating our place since 1921. We had celebrated our Silver Wedding Anniversary, and the restaurant's. In addition to that, I had been working in eating places since my early teens. My whole life had been predicated upon my work—in Italy, in London, and finally

[13]

in America. Now I was leaving; and I confess, as I glanced up and down my street, my eyes were not quite dry.

Well, I thought, I've had some good times on this street—and I've had some bad ones, too, life being what it is. A group of people passed me and went into the restaurant, laughing and talking, their faces flushed and excited. The very sight of them made me feel good; and I thought, I'm going to miss it. I had seen practically a lifetime of opening nights in Sardi's, and yet for some reason each one was every bit as exciting as the one before. I'd never grown tired of the scene. The actors, actresses, producers, and other people connected with the opening night would come and sit in our place to wait for the morning papers to come out with the reviews; some nights there would be celebrations, and some nights they would just get up from their tables and leave, trying their best to look cheerful. Some nights the suspense would be terrible until the papers came, and when they finally did arrive a hush would fall over the room, a silence that seemed to spread even to people who had no stake or interest in the production. Our friends at the New York *Times* had ordered papers to be sent to us the minute they were off the presses, and so we were always the first to find out how a show had gone over. It was the same on nights when shows were opening out of town. Friends would call us from New Haven, Boston, Baltimore, Washington, and sometimes even from as far away as Pittsburgh or Chicago, to let the Sardi crowd know the first-night news. In fact, whenever anything of importance in the entertainment world occurred, Sardi's customers heard about it almost immediately. That even applied to scandal and gossip, I am sorry to say. Years ago, in Hollywood, a famous director and an actress got a little drunk in a cabaret and treated the other guests to an exhibition of lovemaking. An hour or two after it happened, a man in Hollywood telephoned a friend in Sardi's to report it. "That's old stuff," he was told. "We heard about it here twenty minutes ago."

Yes, I thought as I stood there on the sidewalk, I will miss the place—the sense of excitement and exhilaration, the feeling of actual involvement with the living theater, the knowledge that history is being made right under my eyes. I thought of the many productions I had heard discussed in my place, by producers ranging from Winthrop Ames, in the twenties, down to young Mike Sloane and his wife, Paula Stone, who are active on Broadway today. And I thought of other productions—romantic ones, some of which later developed into marriages. I myself never took part in any of the theatrical projects, but as far as the other was concerned, that was something else; I introduced many couples who fell in love and got married. One romance I know I started; it happened the day Claudette Colbert walked in wearing a Red Cross uniform, looking as pretty as a girl in a poster by my old illustrator friend, James Montgomery Flagg. Claudette was working as a volunteer, making collections at a table we set up for her in the lobby. I put a few coins in her collection can and we were standing there, chatting away, when in came a young actor I knew. His name was Norman Foster; he was working in a show across the street. I could see that Claudette caught his eye, so I introduced them. He asked her to lunch; she said she couldn't leave her table. "Will you have lunch with me if I fill up your change can?" he asked. Claudette agreed, and then they sat down. They seemed to get along very well from the beginning, so later, when I heard they were married, I was not at all surprised. As I recall, that marriage ended in a divorce. That was another thing that I learned, soon after becoming a theatrical restaurateur: I had to be careful when inquiring about a husband or a wife, because there seemed to be a high percentage of divorces among people in the entertainment business.

But of course, many marriages survived and endured, and I often wonder if that "high percentage" isn't just a myth invented by the gossip columnists. In fact, a great number of our customers not only stayed married, they raised children and brought them along to Sardi's. I remember Gene Lockhart, the actor and composer, who used to bring in his pretty little daughter, June, who scored a smash hit several seasons ago in *For Love or Money,* a play by F. Hugh Herbert—who, when he is in New York, comes into Sardi's with Diana Herbert, his actress daughter. Marlene Dietrich ate lunch in Sardi's the first day she came to America, bringing her daughter, then a child but now the famous television actress, Maria Riva. The list of parents and children who used to— and still do—eat regularly in our place could fill many pages. J. J. Shubert, of the producing family, ate lunch with us frequently accompanied by his son, Johnny. There was my old friend Leslie Howard, whose life ended tragically in a plane crash; he also used to come to see us often with his son, who is now an actor. Carl Brisson, the Danish cabaret singing star, one day was invited to appear on our radio program, "Luncheon at Sardi's." He asked if it would be all right to bring his daughter-in-law. We said of course, never thinking that she would turn out to be Rosalind Russell, married to Freddie Brisson. Josh White, the ballad singer, has come in many times, bringing his little boy, Josh Jr., who has appeared in a number of Broadway shows. William Gargan and Dennis King, two of my very oldest and best friends, often brought their children in to see us; we watched them grow up along with our own. Once Edith Fellows, who had been a child star, came in with a child of her own; I could hardly believe that she was old enough to have one. Elliott Nugent, the actor and director and writer, used to bring in his daughter, Nancy, who last year appeared with him in a revival of *The Male Animal,* and sometimes he came in with his son-in-law, John Gerstad. (Last year John, too, won acclaim as a director by staging *The Seven-year Itch,* a comedy by George Axelrod, starring another Sardi regular, Tom Ewell.) Eduardo Cianelli, the actor, would show up frequently in the days before he moved to Hollywood, bringing with him his two boys, Ed, Jr., and Lewis, who is now producing movies in Italy. Heywood Broun, the great liberal newspaper columnist, often brought his son, Heywood Hale Broun, Jr., who at first followed his father as a newspaperman and later decided to become an actor. The list could go on and on: there were Ed Wynn and his son Keenan, Frank Craven and his son John, Frank Morgan and daughter Claudia, Oscar Hammerstein and his boy Jimmy, Ken Englund and his stepchildren George and Patsy—those and many, many others all came in. It always made my wife and me proud when our customers brought their children in, for that showed us that they thought of Sardi's as a family place, which was exactly what we tried to make it . . .

Family place, I thought, as the shadows began to stretch along the pavement in 44th Street. Family place: it was a good description, despite the glamour, despite the fame of so many of the customers. And then I began to think of Shirley Booth. She was always like one of our family in the old days. At that time, everybody who knew her was sure that some day she would be a big star and get the acclaim she deserved, but she had a terrible time at first. Parts were scarce, and she was often out of work. Sometimes, when she would get a job, it would be in an out-of-the-way place. Once she took a role with a company that went to a town on Long Island where she and her fellow players had to dress and make up in a jail, because there were no dressing rooms in the hall where the play was put on. Yet she took such jobs without complaining; I never heard her say a word about the theater that wasn't good. As the years went by, her parts became better and better. She appeared in *Three Men on a Horse,* with another old pal of mine, Sam Levene; she was on the radio for a long time in "Duffy's Tavern," and she was a terrific hit as Ruth in the dramatization of Ruth McKenney's *My Sister Eileen.* Yet she never seemed to change in her attitude toward her old friends; she often came to me for advice on various matters, and she always behaved as though

she were our own flesh and blood. (I am glad to say that that
is still the case.) Today Shirley has had almost every honor
that can be given an actress; in 1953 she received both the
Academy Award, for *Come Back, Little Sheba,* and the stage
equivalent, the Antoinette Perry award, for *The Time of the
Cuckoo.* Yet she has not changed one bit. On opening night
of *Come Back, Little Sheba,* she walked into Sardi's after
the performance with her agents, Audrey Wood and William
Liebling. Everybody sitting in the front section stood up and
applauded. Shirley turned around—she didn't even realize
that the ovation was for her! When she opened in *The Time
of the Cuckoo,* which had been written for her especially by
Arthur Laurents, the same thing happened. That day my son
had sent her a telegram and some flowers; the former was
signed, FROM YOUR FAMILY, THE SARDIS. She said to him, "I
loved the flowers, and I love the champagne—but the telegram! Nothing could have made me happier!"

Thinking of Shirley, I was reminded of two actor friends
of hers, Roy Roberts and Barry Thompson. I remembered
how they were always in the place; I don't believe either of
them ever missed a meal in Sardi's any time he was in New
York. One day they complained to me that they couldn't
seem to manage their finances. "I start out trying to save
enough to get through the week, but I always seem to wind
up broke," Roy said. Half as a joke, I made a suggestion.
"Why don't you give me your paychecks, and let me give
you an allowance?" To my surprise, they were delighted with
the idea. So, I opened bank accounts for them, and each
week, when they gave me their checks, I gave them allow-
ances and deposited the rest of their money. When Roy was
ready to go to Hollywood, I showed him his bankbook, and
he couldn't believe that he'd saved so much. After Roy, there
were others who asked me to save money for them, and at
one time some of the boys used to call me the Sardi Bank
and Trust Company . . .

So the memories came back, one following the other, and then I began to recall more old friends: some of them were famous, some were not so well known; some were prosperous, some were down on their luck for long periods. That set me to thinking about the Gloat Club, which used to meet in our place regularly every Thursday afternoon from around 1943 to 1947, or thereabouts. It was composed of Lawrence Langner and Theresa Helburn, of the Theatre Guild, and some of their associates, including, at times, Langner's wife, Armina Marshall, and Jerome Whyte, Agnes De Mille, Rouben Mamoulian, and Richard Rodgers and Oscar Hammerstein. The group called themselves the Gloat Club because they had organized it after *Oklahoma!* was a success. That show is still running—as I write this it is in its tenth year—but there was a time when it looked as though it would never run at all. In fact, at that same time it looked as though the Theatre Guild might have to go out of business, for its affairs were in bad shape. *Oklahoma!* was adapted from Lynn Riggs' play, *Green Grow the Lilacs,* and when the Guild first announced plans for producing it, unexpected trouble arose. Backers simply weren't interested. Everybody advised the Guild against the project. I heard that even the Shuberts were against it—and on Broadway, that ordinarily means certain disaster. Yet Langner and his associates persisted, finally scraped up the money—and the rest of the story is well known. After the play was established as a hit, the producers used to meet in our place to gloat over its unparalleled success. Later the meetings developed into informal discussions of other Guild-Rodgers-Hammerstein productions, such as *Carousel,* another hit, and *Allegro,* which did not do too well. Langner was one of my oldest customers, and I always hoped that he would allow Alex Gard, our caricaturist, to do a drawing for our walls. He refused; he did not like Gard's work, he said, and would not allow his picture to be hung. He said, "Gard is too cruel. Years from now, people who see the Sardi caricatures will conclude that everybody in the theater was a thief, hoodlum, or cutthroat. That may be what some people believe we are, but I don't like to see it suggested so openly!" Another time he said to me, "I might permit a caricature if you will come out to our Westport Playhouse and open a restaurant each summer." I told him what I always told people who made such offers: "This street, 44th Street, is my home, and I don't want to leave it . . ."

Memories like this, I thought, are probably unimportant— they probably wouldn't mean a thing to anyone else, but to my wife and me they are major events. Even the smallest incidents, as they came back, seemed worth remembering, if only because they were connected with friends of long standing. I recalled Paul Whiteman, the bandleader, one of the best patrons of the original Sardi's, whom I'd known when his orchestra had opened at the Palais Royale, one of the great Broadway cabarets of the Twenties. I thought of Bob Ripley, the famous Believe-It-or-Not man, who made his headquarters in Sardi's when he was in New York, and who would send me strange recipes for native dishes when he was traveling around the world. I closed my eyes and saw our dear old friend Josephine Hull, the character actress, who used to walk into our place after every matinee and make a beeline for her favorite table, far off in a corner, where she would sit and catch up on her reading (she always read *The Reader's Digest*) while she was having dinner, attended by Charlie, her favorite waiter. And then I remembered how in those days we had a table in front of the cashier's stand and the cigar counter, where Jenny would eat her lunch and dinner; we called that one The Family Table, but many of our friends liked to sit there because they could talk to Jenny as she sat at the cash register—Antoinette Perry, the director, often used it. Some days she would be joined by John Golden, the producer. He would pretend to be angry because she had taken "his" table, and he would always insist that the only way she could make it up would be by allowing him to pick up her check. They would have a friendly argument, but Mr. Golden almost invariably took the bill. Later, I recall, Miss Perry must have thought that Mr. Golden really was annoyed, for she moved to Table 64, which is still known as Miss Perry's Table. Mr. Golden continued to occupy his usual place, and it was there that he entertained such notables as Bernard Baruch, Mrs. Eleanor Roosevelt, Ex-Ambassador Stanton Griffis, and many others.

Thinking of people who had regular tables, I recalled another good customer of ours, William McChesney Martin, who was known as "the boy president of the Stock Exchange." Around Sardi's, we had another name for him. We called him "Mr. Chocolate." The waiters gave him that name because he never smoked or drank, but always ordered hot chocolate with his dinner. The late Douglas Gilbert, a newspaperman, wrote a story about him, calling it "Mr. Chocolate." Martin enlisted in the army as a private during the war, and worked his way up through the ranks to become an officer. He once wrote me a letter and signed it "Mr. Chocolate." Today he is chairman of the Federal Reserve Board.

But not all my memories were happy ones. I had a few sad ones, too. For years Frank Cavaluzzi was our ice man, coming in day in and day out, never missing a day. He had a big family, and during the war two of his sons went into the service. One day Frank suddenly collapsed and, to our grief and astonishment, died a moment afterward. Within minutes one of his sons came in looking for him. He was home from the army on a pass, and he had not yet seen his father. My Jenny had the anguishing experience of telling the boy what had happened. It affected her deeply, for she had been fond of Frank and his entire family. As a matter of fact it was her nature to take a personal interest in most of the young people who came to eat with us. I remember particularly one young and brilliant lyricist whose songs were later to be hailed far and wide as ranking with the best musical-comedy tunes ever written in this country. My wife treated him like a son. Unfortunately he did not have much will power. He would promise my wife that he was going to stop drinking so much, and then some friends of his would arrive and ask him to sit down, and the next thing he knew he would be drinking again. Some nights when he would fall asleep, exhausted, my wife would make a bed for him in the back of the restaurant.

The recollection of this incident was so real to me it seemed to have happened just a few hours before. Time flies, I thought; and I looked at the place and reflected that it seemed only a short while ago that we had moved in. I remembered the children growing up, and the time when Cino, as a young man in college, decided that he would learn as much as he could about the restaurant business so that he could take over when I would go into retirement. One night he was going to the opera after work. He dressed in white tie and tails at home, then came to the restaurant and changed into his tuxedo coat and black tie to serve dinner. One party kept him busy until it was time for him to leave. When he got to the opera, all dressed in his tails, he thought there was something familiar about the party in the next box. He could not at first recall where he had seen them before. Then he heard them whispering about him and saw them glancing at him from time to time. Finally he recognized one of the men: the party was the same one he had just finished serving in Sardi's! There had been a time, some years before, when my wife and I had thought that Cino might become the actor of the family. I believe it was Frank Craven and Wally Ford who first discovered that he had talent; he was quite a little boy at the time. He appeared in *The Master of the Inn*, which was presented at Winthrop Ames' Little Theatre in 1925, starring Robert Loraine, and featuring Ian Keith, Virginia Pemberton, and Veree Teasdale. He also appeared in two other plays, *Send No Money* and *Buckaroo*, although his part in the latter was cut on opening night. Our daughter Anna was always interested in the theater, too; she had entered Barnard College at fifteen and graduated at nineteen, and she was active in school theatricals all the time she was there. Later, however, she decided that she preferred marriage to a career. Even I was an actor once myself. I was in a movie called *The Worst Woman in Town,* starring Clara Kimball Young. The part was easy for me; I played a captain of waiters in a cabaret. Although it took them all day long to shoot the sequence I was in, it took only a few minutes' time on the screen—and later, when I saw the picture, my whole part had been cut! They made it at a studio in the Bronx, not too far from the apartment my wife and I were renting at the time, so at the end of the day's work I invited the entire cast and crew over to the place for a party. My, how they ate and drank! My wife and I had thought we'd ordered too much food, but by the time those hungry movie people were finished, there wasn't a scrap or drop to be seen in the place. Later I figured it out: the party cost about twice as much as the money I made working in the picture. But I didn't care; we all had a wonderful time.

These thoughts of the children brought back to me the time that Cino went into the marines, during World War II. We were very proud of him, as naturally parents would be, and we were even prouder when our daughter's husband, Frank Gina, also went into the same arm of service. From that time on, all marines, from privates up to generals, always got preferred treatment in Sardi's, as you might imagine. No matter what celebrities or big spenders were waiting in the lobby, the captains and waiters were instructed to give marines the very best tables and to take the best possible care of them. As soon as a marine sat down we automatically gave him a Cherry Point Cocktail, a house specialty made with rum which one of our bartenders invented, named for the base where Cino was stationed. Sometimes, as a joke, I would say to a navy man, "I'll take care of you as soon as I take care of the marines—after all, the navy is part of the marines, isn't it?" They would get upset sometimes, until I would wink and pretend that I'd made a mistake. One night during the war a big, handsome lady marine sergeant came in with a friend. I gave them a good table, and we got to talking. The next night the sergeant came in by herself, this time in evening clothes. At that time Cino and his friend, Captain Newt Crawford, brother of the producer Cheryl Crawford, were home on a week-end leave. I put the lady sergeant next to them. They were very much impressed by her good looks, and all during dinner they kept looking at her, whispering, making jokes. The girl was afraid I would tell them that she was in the marines, but I kept her secret. When she left, Cino asked me who she was. I'll never forget the look of surprise and astonishment on his face when he found out. Except for the marines, however, we never played favorites. We always tried to put certain people at their regular tables, if they came in regularly; I have already mentioned Mr. Golden and Miss Perry and Mrs. Hull, and there were many others—Louis Lotito, head of City Playhouse Corporation, and Mrs. Louise Beck, the widow of Martin Beck, to mention only two—who were always seated in the same positions. And sometimes, I confess, we used to seat certain actors and actresses where they would be on display, so to speak, for many of them seemed to enjoy that. On one or two occasions, we might have put a youngster who needed a job near a table where a producer might have been sitting, on the chance that something might develop. But we always made it a firm rule to admit anybody, regardless of race, creed, or color, and to treat all our customers as though they were the biggest stars or producers in the business . . .

Thus the memories returned as I stood there on the day I retired, the memories and the names: Florence Reed, John and Lionel and Ethel Barrymore, Frank and Ralph Morgan, Sylvia Sidney, Hume Cronyn and Jessica Tandy, Lee Tracy,

Sidney Kingsley, Sam Levene, Broderick Crawford, Jane Cowl, Helen Menken, Helen Keller—I paused in my recollections, remembering the thrill my wife and I had when that great lady first visited us. She later came back again and again, and every visit was a real inspiration to us and to every person in the dining room. (Not long ago she wrote a letter to an acquaintance telling of times when she came to visit us. I hope I will be forgiven if I quote part of it. Miss Keller wrote, "Whenever we entered Mr. Sardi's cosy restaurant, we felt the warmth of his interest not only as a host but also as a friend. I have always loved the expansive, welcoming quality so noticeable in Italian people, and in Mr. Sardi it was all the more winning because of his unusual personality . . . He would bring Mrs. Sardi and his two beautiful children to the table where we sat, and it was a delight to speak with such a handsome family, so appreciative of my teacher, Mrs. Macy, and all she had done to restore me to my human heritage . . . It is refreshing to go over in my memory those gay, carefree hours before I plunged into the work for the blind that has since carried me around the globe. It saddens Miss Thomson [her secretary] and me to think that we have not had leisure to 'fleet the golden time carelessly' at Mr. Sardi's in many a year . . ." I do not have to say how this letter touched my wife and me. As long as we are alive, we will keep it among our most cherished possessions.)

Remembering Miss Keller's sweet face, and the other faces that became so familiar to my wife and me, and recalling the good times, I began to wish that day that I had found time to keep a diary. It would be nice, I thought, if Jenny and I could sit down together and go over an account of the old days, of all the things that happened in Sardi's. Now that I am about to start this new and unfamiliar project, I wish more than ever I had kept a diary. I don't know if these recollections of mine will be of interest; to some they may be meat, to others they may be cafeteria beans. To others, they may not be palatable at all. Some people, although I hope not, may be insulted or hurt because I have forgotten something or omitted a name. I am sure there will be many incidents left out which ought to be included. I offer these memories with the same feeling of uncertainty Jenny and I used to share when we put a new dish on our menu . . .

CHAPTER TWO

Il Vagabondo

IT WAS ONE TERRIFIC CELEBRATION. The village was a tiny one, so tiny it could scarcely have been called even a hamlet, and when the people had something to celebrate, they did it right. Out came the finest and most colorful clothes— the men wearing their best white homespun linen shirts and brown corduroy trousers, the women trying on their prettiest scarves and their laciest petticoats; out came the fiddles, the accordions, and the guitars, and out came big Duca, the clarinetist, who always led the musicians; and out came the finest wines and the richest foods. Oh, it was a great party: it raged up and down the streets, in and out of houses, up and down the streets again, and some of it even ran over to the adjoining towns. Everybody sang and danced and drank and ate and kissed each other; everybody was in an hilarious holiday mood.

I slept through it all, I am sorry to say. Occasionally I awoke to complain, but not often. When I did, nobody paid much attention. At a party that lasts three whole days, who has time for the guest of honor?

No, the sad truth is that I had nothing to do with my party, for it began when I was only a few hours old. It happened on December 23, 1885, in the small, beautiful village of San Marzano Oliveto, in the Piemonte region of the province of Alessandria, in Italy. I was later told that I came into the world at eleven o'clock at night. The party began shortly thereafter and did not wind up until the baptismal ceremony, more than seventy-two hours later. I have always been regretful that I wasn't old enough to join in, but I console myself when I think that I have seen a good many parties in my restaurant since that time.

If I had been able to participate in that first celebration, or even if I had been able to make myself understood, I believe I might have had something to say about the names they gave me. My mother had been Anna Gilardino. She had married Giovanni Sardi, and I was their first son. There was a custom of long standing in that branch of the Sardi family to which my father belonged. Each of the preceding three generations had produced three boys, and each son had been named for one of the Three Kings, the celebrated biblical Wise Men. Because my paternal grandfather had been named Melchiorre, so was I. One of my uncles, Pio, became my godfather, and I was also given his name. Then, finally, my mother's side of the family had to be represented. Since her mother's name was Vincenza, they gave me the masculine counterpart, Vincenzo. Thus I bore a name which, at that age, I could not have lifted: Melchiorre Pio Vincenzo Sardi. Later they gave me a nickname, the diminutive of Vincenzo; in English, I suppose it would be spelled Cencin, both c's being pronounced as "ch." When I got to America, I called myself Vincent. My wife and I gave our son this name, too, but we have always called him by another diminutive, Cino. (Just to mix things up more, he prefers to be called "Vincent.")

As I grew older, I was known by another name in the villages in which my family lived. It was one they gave me because of my nature and disposition. I was not a very good boy, I am afraid, and if you come right down to it, I suppose I was actually bad. I was so bad that I am sure if they had known how I was going to be, they would have gone into mourning instead of celebrating my birth. Looking at it one way, I even proved to be obstreperous before I was born. Everybody in the family had been hoping that I might arrive on Christmas Day, in which case they would have called me Natale, or perhaps Natalino. But, no, I came on the twenty-third, against their wishes. And later, I kept on in the same way. I could never seem to do what they wanted me to. Because I was rebellious, always playing pranks, always getting in trouble, always running away from home, always acting the renegade, they called me The Vagabond, or *Il Vagabondo*. The name stuck. Years later, whenever I saw people from my old village, they would exclaim, "Well, how is The Vagabond?"

In the theater and the movies it always makes a better story if the main character is born poor, leads an honest and virtuous life during boyhood, studies hard, obeys and honors his parents, and by doing all this winds up in a prominent position. I make no claims about the position I am in today. I doubt that my name will ever be in any history books, except those on the contemporary theater which might be written by George Jean Nathan, Richard Watts, or Brooks Atkinson. All I have done in my life is run a restaurant which happened to be a place where people of the stage and screen came to eat and visit with each other. I knew most of my customers by name, liked most of them, had a good time taking care of them, and tried to help them whenever I could. Now that I have retired and the place is being operated by my son, they are still in it, the ones who are alive—and the others have been replaced by a generation of his age or a little younger. But I did not get to the place I am in today, whatever it is, by following the movie formula. As a boy, I hardly ever studied. My life was by no means virtuous; as I have mentioned above, I was in a constant commotion with my parents. Nor was I born poor. On the contrary, my family was quite well-to-do when I was a child. But before I tell about my family, let me describe the land in which we lived.

The Piemonte section is one of the loveliest in all of Italy. Set in the northwestern part, it is a country of rolling hills, striped with long rows of grape vines, broken up by small wooded copses, laced here and there by little streams, and steeped in the light of a sun that seems to shine more brightly on Italy than on any other land. The earth is rich. The wheat grows tall, and the fat, juicy grapes bend the vines to the ground. Naturally, people who live there are mainly farmers. The wine they produce is known all over the world.

My father's branch of the Sardi family had lived in the Piemonte for many, many generations. The family was respected and influential; one of my father's cousins, a general, was an aide to King Umberto. Originally my father's home had been in Canelli, a town a few miles from San Marzano, but at the time I was born he was employed as overseer of a large estate belonging to the Parodi, a wealthy family of Genovese bankers. The Parodi maintained an enormous tract of land on which stood a castle surrounded by many farms. They occupied the castle only in the summer, but my father looked after the entire estate the year around. This was quite a task, for the Parodi practically owned the village. (Now, there is a funny coincidence that ought to go in here, and this is what it is: a good friend of ours, particularly of my son's, is Alfred Drake, the star of *Oklahoma!* and *Kiss Me, Kate.* Alfred is of Genovese ancestry. Not long ago, when he heard me talking of the Parodi, he said he thought he was related to them through his mother! It is a smaller world than any of us thinks!)

Each of the farms around the castle was occupied by two tenant families, who kept their own livestock and raised crops, dividing the profits with the Parodi. My father saw to it that these tenants kept their places in good condition, and also had in his charge a carpenter, several men to look after horses and carriages, a blacksmith, painters, supervisors, and paymasters, as well as numerous household servants who worked in the castle. One of my earliest memories has to do with those household servants. When I had done something mischievous, I was punished by being sent to eat with them in the kitchen. To me, this was not a punishment at all; I loved the happy atmosphere out there, and I used to look forward to eating with the help.

My father was the best looking and best educated of three handsome and cultured brothers. One went to Milano and married an actress, scandalizing the family; my grandfather Sardi gave him some money and told him never to come back, so I don't remember too much of him. Another married my mother's sister and went into the wine business; he was a good-hearted soul, something of a sport, and he could not seem to settle down. My father went to college and continued his studies to the end of his days; I can still see him reading by a dim lamp in the evenings after supper. He was a soft-spoken, gentle man, loved by all in his command; as far back as I can remember, I never heard him raise his voice in anger or give a sharp order. He loved birds, and his well-stocked aviary included canaries, lovebirds, cardinals, a parakeet, and some rare specimens from Australia. One day a favorite bird escaped and was shot by one of the farmers by mistake. My father was sad, but he did not rebuke the man.

There is no question that my mother was the dominating force in my early life—and, indeed, in the life of everyone in our family. I don't remember my father ever beating me; it was always my mother. In later years when I wrote home, I addressed her; she was a big woman, and she ruled the family. Her people, the Gilardinos, had been merchants who had worked hard and accumulated considerable wealth, and at the time she married my father her family was as powerful in that section as his was. Her grandfather had owned many highly productive vineyards, and her parents had made their money in the dry-goods business. One brother had also been very successful in this line.

Soon after I was born, my mother became expectant again. In those days babies were always breast-fed; the parents did not know about bottles, formulas, Pablum, and strained baby foods as mothers do today. The child was suckled until his teeth came in, and then he was given adult foods. Many things were done crudely. The village barber was also the dentist. When you had a toothache, he would swab your gum with antiseptic, take a pair of pliers, and whoosh! pull it out, dabbing the wound with cotton. If a man had a black-and-blue bruise or was suffering from high blood pressure, the doctor would bring a leech to suck him. Oh, how I hated to see that doctor coming! He covered many villages and made his rounds on horseback. Whenever I saw him coming down over the hill, I ran to hide. My mother didn't summon him often; she had a good many home remedies she brewed from herbs which the servants gathered in the surrounding countryside. I didn't mind those medicines much; the one I hated was the one all children hate: castor oil. But now I am getting away from my story.

Naturally, when my mother was expecting again, she could no longer breast-feed me, so they took me away and gave me to a wet nurse. This woman was a big, healthy farmer's wife who lived on a nearly inaccessible place set in the woods high up in the hills, nearer to Canelli than to San Marzano. I was too tiny to know exactly what was going on, but I am told that I cried as they took me away.

Because of the other child, I was kept with the wet nurse a long time. When I was brought back home, my mother had given her breast to the new baby. I knew that I had been replaced, and it made a difference to me. Although the farmer's wife had been a good, kindly woman, it had not been the same, and I don't suppose I ever completely recovered from the experience as long as I was a child.

I am not an educated man. While others in my family were going to school for their formal learning, I was washing dishes in a London restaurant. But I know enough of human nature to realize that that early experience made a vivid, lasting impression. Perhaps it accounts for some of the impishness and restlessness I showed later on. Certainly the rest of my brothers and sisters were more normal and better behaved. There were three sisters—Matilda, Luigia, and Elena; and two brothers, Eduardo and Domenico. Of the whole family, Domenico was my favorite. Maybe it was because in some ways he and I were like each other, and had been from babyhood (he, too, had been brought up by a wet nurse). He was restless and mischievous, too. When he grew older, he decided that he did not want to be a priest, as the family had ordained, and he became an actor. Now, this was quite a serious thing in those days, because there was always a great war between the church and the stage. Yet although you might say that almost every third door along any street in Canelli belonged to a relative of ours, I never heard a bad word against Domenico. He was always broke, he was always irresponsible, he was always traveling away, he was always giving his money to less fortunate friends; and everybody loved him. He was very popular with the girls—he was so handsome, they called him the Maurice Costello of Italy— but all the men liked him, too. Often he would show up late for a rehearsal and the director would bawl him out, but then he would make a joke and the director would not be angry any more. I often wish that I had seen him on the stage, but I never had that opportunity. Marta Abba, the actress, told me once that she had played with him in Italy, but she could not remember where. He was a great favorite in Milano and Torino, but he played in theaters all over Italy and once went down to Africa with a company. He died suddenly of a acute attack of appendicitis in 1937. My other brother and my sisters are still living. Elena is now in this country, happily married to Attilio Scoffone, my favorite brother-in-law. Eduardo, who came over with me, is here too, but never married.

When I finally was taken from the wet nurse I was quite

a stranger to my family and the household, although there
was one person who looked after me. Her name was Louisa,
and she had been a maid in the service of my grandfather
Sardi. In those early years she was like a mother to me. She
took it upon herself to be my protector. So did another maid
we had, Carlotta, and her husband, Giuseppe, who was our
stableman. Giuseppe was in charge of all the horses, some of
which were used for riding, some for carriage work, and some
in the fields. I spent most of my days in the stable, hanging
around watching Giuseppe and the other men, and in time
I learned to swear the way they did. I also learned another
lesson, this one more constructive. I forget how old I was;
five or six, if I am not mistaken. I cut myself some sticks
and made a bow and arrow, and in order to see how sharp
it was, I went up to a horse that was tied outside the stable.
Going around to her rear, I took careful aim and pinked
her in the rump. She reared, plunged, and kicked out. Her
knee caught me, and I went down on the ground. I scrambled
to my feet and ran like mad to the church next door, where
I prayed and doused myself with holy water all over. I think
I even drank some of it to get my breath back. Well, God
did help me, because I was not hurt seriously and nobody
ever found out about it. Since that day I have always had
confidence in divine power, and there have been many times
in my life when I have prayed, and how!

I suppose that recollections of early childhood are jumbled
together in most people's minds—or perhaps I am saying that
only because mine is no exception. My memory actually begins from the age of about seven or eight, when I began to
go to school. First I went to public school in San Marzano.
The teacher there was a lady who had only one arm, and we
used to make her life miserable. Sometimes we would steal
her lunch, put pepper in her food, or hide her books and
pencils. The school was in the city hall, and we often annoyed her so much that she would call on the mayor to dis-
cipline us. He would come in and speak to us, and then we

would behave for a while. Other times, in winter, she had a worse punishment for us. There was a good deal of snow around there; often we had to wade through drifts above our knees. The teacher would go around the room and single out the children who hadn't washed their ears, and she would make them go out and bring in snow and wash with that. It always happened that the bad ones had dirty ears. It made you feel good afterward, but not while you were doing it! As in every other country, the custom in Italy in those days was for the teacher to keep the bad pupils after school for an hour or two. There were few times when I got home on time.

That teacher was glad to see me leave San Marzano, but her pleasure was nothing like that of the local priest, Don Costa. He was bald, and he seemed to me to be at least a hundred years old. He wore a toupee. Whenever I could, I would snitch it from him and hide it, and sometimes he could not find it for days on end.

A year or two after I started school the Parodi suffered a financial setback. They were forced to sell their estate in San Marzano, and it was cut up into separate, smaller properties. This left nothing for my father to do there, and so he retired and our family moved back to Canelli. Thus I have always thought of Canelli as my home town, the place where I belong, and I have few memories of San Marzano. One of my sisters and my brother Eduardo and I had preceded the family back to Canelli, so that we could attend school there. We stayed with Louisa, the maid, in the house of my Uncle Gustavo, one of my father's brothers. It was no ordinary house; today, in fact, it is the Palazzo Municipale (or City Hall). This time poor Louisa had her hands full—not because of my brother or sister, but because of *Il Vagabondo*, who was always raiding the cupboard, getting into fights with neighboring children, or looking for trouble of some other kind. Each week Louisa would make a full report to Mama Sardi, and then the brush, stick, quirt, or hand would fall upon *Il Vagabondo* in the usual place. It happened so regularly that I almost became immune.

A few years ago I went back to Canelli. It had not changed much since my boyhood. The cobblestone streets were as I remembered them, and so was the dusty village square. The shops around the square were the same—the butcher's, the drugstores, the baker's, and the hardware shop all were as I had pictured them. I felt wistful when I saw them, for I knew those places well; you see, whenever I ran away from home, which was often, I would first go to one of the stores. The merchants were my friends; the whole village adopted me, you might say. The first thing I always did when I ran away was to go to one of the storekeepers and charge some bread and cheese and salami to my father's account, and then I would take these provisions with me while I hid out in the hills. Sometimes I would stay away four, five, or even ten days at a time—in the summer. In the winter I didn't seem to run away as often.

The trouble was, I wasn't able to keep my mind either on studies or work. Whenever I picked up a book, I would read for a while and then find that my eyes hurt. The teacher always punished me when I did not know my lessons. To get even, I would spill ink, or make a noise while somebody else was reciting. Then I would be punished again and I would run away. When I got back home, of course, I would be punished a second time. After some time my mother decided to put a stop to it.

"Cencin," she said to me one day, "we have decided to send you away to school."

I said nothing; I didn't know if that would be good or bad.

"As you know," she continued, "it has always been the custom in the Sardi family for the oldest boy to be a priest."

Now I began to get scared. I didn't want to be a priest. It looked to me as though they never had any fun.

"Your father has made arrangements for you to go to Don Bosco," my mother said. "You will leave next week."

I went out and hung around the stable for a while. I was so angry I could hardly talk. When Giuseppe asked me what the trouble was, I did not even speak to him. That evening I tried to tell them I didn't want to go, but I never got a chance to explain my point of view. Their minds were made up.

Don Bosco, or Dunwoody College, was located in Varazze, in the province of Liguria, near Genoa. The priests were very strict. When I arrived, I was given the official welcome —that is, someone handed me a uniform and someone else showed me the bed where I was to sleep.

"What kind of a place is this?" I asked a boy whose bed was near mine.

He did not answer; he held his nose. It did not take long for me to find out that I agreed with him. Everything at Dunwoody was regimented, like a military school, maybe even worse. That regimentation did not appeal to me. We were awakened early in the morning and sent immediately to mass. Then came breakfast, and then long hours in hot, uncomfortable classrooms, after which we had a small lunch and more classes. After that was a short play period, then supper, and a study hour. On my first evening there, a terrific electrical storm arose. Some of us were outside; we ran against the wall to get under the sheltering eaves, but we stood too close to a wire that ran down from a lightning rod. The lightning struck the rod with a tremendous crack, and a ball of fire rolled down and vanished into the ground. Some of us were thrown down by it. I wished I was home.

Our main exercise at Dunwoody consisted of marching into the country, led by the younger priests. That might not have been so bad if we hadn't had to march like soldiers, but I didn't like the routine at all. I would always sneak out of line and run off into the fields to steal the olives, lemons, and other fruit that grew around there. Every time I did it they caught me, and every time I was punished by being sent to bed without my supper. On the next hike, however, I would try it again.

Then too, there was the salt situation. Salt in Italy in those days was controlled by the state and very expensive. At home, since we were fairly well off, we had always used it liberally on food, and I had not known how it was to be without it. But at Dunwoody the frugal priests cooked the boys' food entirely without salt. I couldn't stand it. One day one of my friends told me that the faculty always had salt with meals. I resolved that I would get some of it. In my stockinged feet, I sneaked into the faculty dining room and stole some salt. I did it during a rest period, and I was certain that nobody saw me, but someone did, and I was reported and punished once more.

That settled it for me. The only thing I knew to do was to run, so I did—but, of course, they caught me. I tried it again, and again I was caught. That time the priests decided that they had had enough, too. They sent for my parents to come and take me back home.

Now my real troubles began. They got so bad I even wished on occasion that I was back at Dunwoody. My parents were very disappointed at my disgrace.

"Now," said my mother, "since you won't go to school, you must work around here."

My oldest sister had gone to help out at my grandfather's dry-goods store, and since we were not as prosperous as we had been when my father worked for the Parodi, we did not have the servants of previous days. With my sister gone, much of the housework fell to me to do—I had to make the beds, shine shoes, and get up in the early morning to start the breakfast. Meanwhile, my brother Eduardo could run about and play as freely and happily as he wanted to. "I'm not built for being nailed to a sink," I used to say to myself. They also made me serve as altar boy to the priest at our local church, and I did not like that chore, either. On top of all this, they sent me back to the Canelli school.

From time to time I would catch Eduardo or one of my sisters and force them to help me do the dirty work, but whenever I did they told my mother, and I don't have to say what happened then. Oh, I remember how often I used to stand at the sink, washing dishes, wishing I was out with the other boys my own age, playing ball or marbles; or helping my side in a fight! It was pure torture and finally I grew tired of that diet. One night I simply sneaked out of the house while everybody was asleep and walked to a town a few miles from Canelli where some relatives lived.

"Hello, Cencin, what brings you here?" asked the head of the house (I believe he was a cousin of my mother's).

"Why," I said, with a straight face, "Mother is sick, so they sent me here for a few days."

That seemed to satisfy him—or so I thought. What happened was that he waited until he could notify my family. They had no telephones then, and word had to be sent by someone going to Canelli. Meanwhile, I was enjoying myself there, eating excellent meals and being thankful that I didn't have to work. A day or two later, when I realized that the relative was sending a message to my folks, I moved on to another town, and told another set of relatives the same story. I did this several times until I ran out of relatives.

Each time I was taken home, things were no better than before. The more they scolded, the worse I got. The worse I got, the more I was punished. The more I was punished, the more I ran away. Sometimes, taking a cue from what I had done when I was younger, I would run first to the store, stock up with food on my father's account, and stay in the hills for nearly a month. There I would tramp around, hunt birds, and do a little fishing. I would sometimes catch and kill a mess of little larks and roast them over a fire, eating them head, feathers, legs, and all. (Years later, in my restaurant, Paul Whiteman told me that he had enjoyed birds done this way, with *polenta,* that corn-meal mush cake so popular with many Italian families. Once I got hold of six dozen Egyptian quail, each no bigger than a sparrow, and we roasted them for Paul in a casserole with rosemary. A big man, he had a bigger appetite, and he ate them, every one.)

On colder nights when I ran away, I would always make sure to leave one door to the house open, and then I would sneak in and make a bed in a storage room where old furniture was kept. Soon the family got wise to this, and they would bolt the door when they knew I had gone. When that happened, I took to climbing into the attic; our house was set against a hill, and all I had to do was to run up the side to get in a window. One night my father heard me up there. I could hear him speak to my mother. "What's that?" he cried.

"It must be a cat," she said.

"I'll go see," my father said.

By the time he reached the attic, I had skinned out the window and climbed up on the roof. I slept up there that night, straddling the peak of the roof, my legs hanging down on either side. The next morning my mother saw me and almost fainted. "Come down!" she cried. I would not have thought of disobeying, so down I went—but I did not go to her. I went off into the hills again and stayed away a couple of days.

My whole family just about gave me up as a hopeless case. Among all our relatives, I had only one friend, Uncle Pietro Gilardino. He is dead now, but his kindness to me has been a sort of guiding light all my life—he was the only one who seemed to understand that I did not mean to be bad and that I meant no harm. Because he was so good to me, I always did everything he asked me to. I spent a great deal of time around his place—he had a big winery—and in return for doing small jobs he allowed me to go about his stables as much as I pleased. I had always loved horses, and I was particularly fond of a beautiful little one called Balin, or Buckshot. Uncle Pietro did not allow me to drive Buckshot in town, but I could sit beside the driver, and when we reached the country he would let me take the reins in my hands. It seemed to me that there was no greater pleasure in the world. Yet I was not satisfied. I wanted to drive that horse all by myself, without the driver. It became a passion with me. I had to do it. There must have been something in me that made me want to disobey even Uncle Pietro, my patron. So, one day when the driver had dismounted to attend to some business in a store, I grabbed the reins and whipped up Buckshot. I drove all over town, proud as a duke—until Uncle Pietro's man caught me. I don't have to tell the aftermath of that adventure. After that, even Uncle Pietro washed his hands of me for a time.

Having lost him as a protector, I went back to my old habits. I kept running away, and they kept catching me and punishing me.

"This cannot go on any longer," I heard my mother say to my father one day.

"Yes, you're right, we must do something about the boy," my father said, in his customary gentle voice.

I thought, Well, I guess I'd better run away again. But just then I heard something that interested me.

". . . on a ship," a voice said. I don't know whose voice it was; that of an uncle, more than likely.

"Yes, yes, perhaps a ship," my father said. He sounded troubled.

It was clear to me immediately. They were thinking of sending me away to a sailing ship; that was what families did to incorrigible boys in those days. I decided not to run away, after all. The prospect of going aboard a real ship was fascinating. If I had known what I was in for, however, I would have run so far away they never would have caught me.

CHAPTER THREE

The Reluctant Sailor

W HAT'S YOUR NAME, BOY?" the big man asked. He was
tall, with the wind- and sun-burned skin of the mariner,
but although his voice was rough he seemed friendly.

I was soaked to the skin, and although the sun was shin-
ing I was shivering, and my teeth were chattering. "S-s-sardi,"
I managed to stammer.

"Your first name, boy," he said.

"Cencin," I said. "V-v-vincenzo."

"Don't you know better than to fall into the water?" he
demanded.

"I come from up north," I said. "I never saw so much
water before."

"Where in the hills?"

"Piemonte." I jumped up and down a little to try to warm
my shaking body.

"Go down and get warm, Piemonte," he said. "Change
your clothes."

"I haven't got any clothes," I said. "They won't come from
home until tomorrow."

"Well, see if you can warm up then and dry those off, Piemonte," he said, and walked away. His name, I later learned,
was Ernesto Lavagnini, and he was the first mate on the ship,

[42]

a three-masted schooner called *Melina.* Although he seemed like a kind man, I was already convinced that I didn't like the life of a sailor.

The day before, after I'd said good-by to my brothers and sisters and my father, my mother and I had set out on the longest trip I'd ever taken. We traveled all night long and most of the day, and finally arrived in the seaport town of La Spezia.

Originally my parents had thought to send me to a ship operated by a Captain Caraventa. This ship was a sort of reform school for bad boys; it was so bad that Caraventa's own brother, who knew our family, suggested that they would not want to send me there, no matter how troublesome I was. One of the bartenders who works for us now in the restaurant, Mario, was on that Caraventa ship as a boy. From what he has told me, I am glad my family changed their minds.

Another relative had heard of this new berth for me. In La Spezia, he told my parents, there was a Captain D. Lena, who was in the wine business. He was a good businessman who owned three English schooners. They sailed up and down the coast of Italy, around the toe of the boot, to Sicily, and sometimes ranged as far as Marseilles, in France. Their cargo was mostly wine, cheese, olive oil, and olives, and other native products. My family got in touch with Captain Lena and asked if he had need of a good strong boy to work in return for his food. They were not exaggerating when they said I was strong; I was big for my age, and my life outdoors while running away from home had toughened me. Captain Lena was very glad to take up the family's offer, and so, without any more discussion, my mother and I had set out on the long trip.

At La Spezia she had got in touch with Captain Lena immediately, and after a few minutes of conversation we had gone with him to the dock, where he had signaled to the schooner waiting at anchor out in the harbor. Soon I saw a rowboat push out from the side and start for the shore.

Our parting was very short. "I hope you will behave your-self," my mother said.

"Yes," I said.

"I hope you will learn to be a better boy," she said.

"Yes," I said.

"Remember to say your prayers," she warned.

"I will," I promised.

She kissed me, I kissed her back, and then she went away. I think I saw a tear in her eye, and to tell the truth, there may have been one or two in mine. She had promised that the rest of my clothes, which had been sent by a different route, would arrive the next day. I hopped into the boat, eager for my first experience on the water. As we pulled away from the dock, I thought I could see my mother's figure walking down a street toward the center of the town. I felt no pangs. This is what they want me to do, I thought; and, as I have said, I was looking forward to life aboard the *Melina*. From what I had read, a sailor's life sounded as though it would just suit me. I was about eleven and a half years old.

Shortly after that I changed my mind.

When we got out to the ship, the man who had rowed me scrambled right up the wooden stairs that had been let down. Halfway up, he turned. "Come on, boy."

I did not want to go. I was busy with the water, splashing my hands in it, looking for fish, pulling on the oars, trying to see my reflection on the moving wavelets. I pretended that I didn't hear him, and he went on up to the deck. After a time I thought I would go after him. I reached out to grasp the rope to pull myself up onto the steps, but in doing so I pushed the rowboat further away. Suddenly, with a quick-ness that took my breath away, I found myself in the water! I gasped, and the water seemed to fill my body. I went under, thrashing around, and I was sure I was going to die. I closed my eyes and felt myself come above the water, but when I gasped for air I got more water in my lungs. I tried to shout for help, and the same thing happened. Then I felt something cut into my neck, and I must have fainted. The next thing I knew something was striking my face, and when I opened my eyes I saw that I was being slapped. I threw up a lot of water and, weakened, fell down on the deck. They had pulled me out by the neck.

A group of sailors were standing around watching, laughing as though my performance had been the funniest thing they'd ever seen. "So," one shouted, "the *mozzo* (greenhorn) thought he would go swimming, eh?" They all laughed again. I hated them, all of them, but I was too weak and cold and still too frightened even to shake my fist. That was when Lavagnini asked me my name and where I was from. Because he was the only one who treated me like a human being, I felt drawn to him. Later he became my protector and saved my life.

It did not take me long to learn that there was nothing romantic about a sailor's life as I was ordered to lead it. Captain Lena was a kind man, not as friendly as his first mate, but kind enough—but he had sent for me in order to get a new pair of hands, and he expected full use of them. I had thought that my day was full at Dunwoody College, but I now realized that going there had been like a vacation.

I was on the go from morning till night, and because I was big, they expected me to do a man's work. In fact, they started me polishing brass around the deck the very day I arrived, even before I had a chance to dry off. Believe me, I felt foolish, working in that soaking-wet suit! But polishing brass was almost the easiest of my chores. Every dirty job on the *Melina* fell to me. I washed dishes in the galley, and when I did not do a good job, the cook would give me a clout on the ears. I cleaned the cabins and kept the captain's quarters in order.

On top of that, I had to do more than a man's work when the *Melina* put into port. Captain Lena would buy wine at one port and put it in great vats in the hold. Then, at other ports we visited, the buyers would come and taste the wine and order a certain number of barrels. We would pump it from the vats into barrels and row it ashore. I usually had to row a boatful of barrels myself, and when I reached the dock I would have to lift them up. Each one weighed—oh, I am sure they weighed at least two hundred pounds, and sometimes I would row ten or eleven of them at one time. It was back-breaking work. Several times I considered running away, but to tell the truth, I didn't know where I would go. Also, I was afraid of what they would do to me if they caught me. They were all rough and tough. Whenever I managed to get by for an hour without getting a kick or a good punch, I thought I was lucky. Sometimes they did it just to hear me howl, not because I had done anything wrong or bad.

Many times, after a long, hard day's work, I had to stand watch. The watch was four hours at a time, and I was usually so tired that I couldn't stay awake. The first time I tried the watch I fell asleep, and was awakened by one of the sailors hitting me. He took me to the captain.

"You must stay awake, boy," the captain said.

"But I'm tired," I said. "I can't keep my eyes open."

"You must," he said. "Try whistling to keep yourself awake. If we catch you asleep again, you will be punished." He gave the sailor a significant look. That man seemed eager to help me stay awake. I managed it for that watch, but the next night when I tried to keep my eyes open, I couldn't. They caught me sleeping and beat me. The night after that, I stole some hardtack from the galley. The cook caught me and gave me a swat, but I ran away with my pockets full of hardtack, and I chewed it all through my watch. That time I didn't fall asleep, so from then on I knew that hardtack-chewing would be my solution.

I was never seasick while out on a voyage; I was only sick of the sea and the work. They made me tar the ropes and scrape the mast. Because everybody else did, I learned to go barefoot; in fact, I believe they took away my shoes. I don't imagine that anybody ever had as much trouble going barefoot as I did. It seemed that no matter how careful I was, I always stumbled over something and stubbed my toe. Half the time I was jumping around on one foot, holding the injured member. When I climbed the mast, I often got painful splinters in my hands and feet. One day while we were in a port I was up there scraping the mast, the main one, high at the top, when a sudden electrical storm came up. Down on the deck, everybody ran for cover. I had always been a little afraid of storms since the day at Dunwoody when the lightning struck the rod near me, and I was in a hurry to get down from that mast. In my haste I slipped and lost my grip. The first stop down was the crow's nest. I bounced off that and fell all the rest of the way, from rope to yardarm and back to rope, and when I hit the deck I heard a terrific *crack!* I must have passed out, for when I woke up they had me in the hospital, and they told me my leg had been splintered and an ankle broken. I was in that hospital three weeks or more, and it was a great treat! For one thing, it was the first time I'd slept between nice, clean sheets since going on the boat. For another thing, I didn't have to work; and for another, the food was wonderful.

The food on the *Melina* had been like shipboard food everywhere in those days: awful. We used to get dried beans, smoked fish, rice, spaghetti, and tomato paste. We never had fruit or vegetables, and I don't believe we saw meat more than once a month. As was the Italian custom, we always had wine with our meals, but we never drank it from a glass— they used to pass around a bottle with a spout at the end, and we held it up and squirted it in our open mouths. We had some coffee with each meal, but it was bitter, and there was no cream for it—only a small lump of brown sugar.

Compared to that, the hospital fare was heavenly. Lying there, I decided I had had enough of the sea. I thought again of running away, but then I remembered that my leg was still in the cast and splint. Well, I thought, I will go as soon

as it gets better. Before I could do that, Captain Lena came
and got me, and I was back on board the *Melina* again.

Whenever we put in at a port, I would row in with my
wine barrels, but I was always under strict instructions to return to the ship. Also, there was always somebody there on the
dock to see that I followed those instructions. Then, when I
came back, practically the entire crew, including the captain
and the mate, would take off for a brief holiday in the town,
leaving me on the ship and taking away all the small boats
so I couldn't follow. I believe I would have gone half-crazy
with loneliness if it hadn't been for a mongrel dog I'd
adopted. I called him Tiger, and he was my best friend. I
used to sit and talk to him while they were all away. When
the men started to come back, I would always hide. They
were generally drunk, and they thought it was great sport to
catch Piemonte and kick him or hit him to make him yell.

Once, while they were all ashore, I thought I would have
myself a kind of picnic. I went to the galley and got some
bread and cheese. This time, I thought, I will not drink my
wine out of that bottle with the spout. So I went to the captain's quarters to get a glass. Down in the galley, as I was
pouring my wine, the ship tossed suddenly. The glass broke
against the bottle and a huge, jagged hunk fell and cut my
bare toe. Blood spurted everywhere. I was really frightened.
I dragged myself up to the deck, the blood flowing after me
in a trail. Down beside the ship was a small rowboat which
for some reason they had not taken into the port. I skinned
down the rope, sat in the boat, and held my foot in the water
to stop the bleeding. It only seemed to bleed all the more,
and the water turned red. The sight of it made me sick, and
I passed out. When I came to, I felt a pain in my foot the
like of which I'd never felt before. It was almost unbearable.
They had found me and were sewing up the cut. It took
three stitches. Of course, there was nothing like an anesthetic
aboard the *Melina*. I still carry the scar from that accident.

After I had been on the ship for a while things were a

little better. The men seemed to get used to me. I think it may have been because I did as hard a day's work as any of them. They would still hit me whenever they had the chance, some of them, but it was not by any means as bad for me as it had been. Also, I became better at ducking.

There was one man I never could get along with, however, and he almost did away with me. His name was—well, never mind what his name was. Call him Santo. He was a big, burly man with an uncouth manner. He had worked on English ships, and on them he had learned to curse and swear in English. Most of the other sailors swore a lot, but I was used to that because of the words I'd learned from the stablemen back home. But this Santo, whenever he swore at me for something, used English words which I did not understand.

One day, after he had called me a phrase that he used often, I went to see one of my friends among the crew and repeated it for him as nearly as I could. "What does it mean?" I asked.

"It means that your mother was a dog," he said, laughing.

I hit the ceiling, I was so mad. "What, he's saying my mother was a dog?" I demanded.

"That's what it means," the friend said.

"I'll get even with him for that," I said.

The truth is that Santo was so big and tough I was afraid of him, a little, and so I did not go right to where he was and pick a fight. I told myself I would wait. But my temper was boiling. I have always been able to keep my temper, but when I can't keep it any longer it gets fierce.

A day or two later, while I was polishing some brass near the captain's cabin, this Santo came by on the deck. He sneered at me and called me the name again.

I saw red. I was holding a screw driver which I had been using to unscrew some brass fixtures, so as to clean them better. Holding it like a knife, I leaped straight at him, try-ing to stab him in the face. He was so surprised, he almost forgot to dodge. The screw driver just went by his cheek, scratching his face. Then he recovered and grabbed me. First he knocked me down with his fists, and then he kicked me. He had a temper, too. He picked me up off the deck and took me over to the side of the boat, to the railing. A bunch of the sailors saw him and ran up and stopped him. If they hadn't, I would have been drowned for sure. He dropped me on the deck. I lay there sobbing. I am sure he would have kicked me again if it hadn't been for the others taking him away. He looked down at me and said, "You better stay away from me, you——" and he called me the name again. "Some day I get you."

I had thought he would let it go at that, but I was mistaken. A couple of days later, while we were far out at sea, I was standing by the rail. The deck was almost deserted. The next thing I knew, he was sneaking toward me. Once again he grabbed me, and once again he was ready to throw me overboard, but this time the mate, Lavagnini, caught him in the act. Lavagnini made Santo put me down, and then he put the bully in solitary confinement until we got to port. There Santo was discharged from the crew, and I never saw him again. As anybody could imagine, I wasn't very sorry to see him go.

Lavagnini became my only real friend on the boat. He was a family man, and once when we returned to La Spezia he took me along to visit his wife and children for a week end. They lived in Fezzano, a little town not too far away. They treated me so well that when I went to bed that night I cried a little, for I suddenly realized that I was homesick for my family. I had not heard much from them while I was on the boat, and I was just about certain that they had forgotten me. In order to keep from feeling too bad, I had decided that I would not think about them any more. I never forgot Lavagnini's kindness. I kept up a correspondence with him for a long time. Years later, when I returned from America to Italy on a visit, I went to see him. That was in 1925. The poor fellow, he was all crippled up with rheumatism—but he

recognized me, and he cried like a father welcoming his long-
lost son. I confess that I cried a little too, but then we had a
nice conversation. He died a few months afterward; I cor-
responded with his wife for a long time, but she, too, died
after World War II.

One day, after I had been on the ship over a year and a
half, I had a pleasant surprise when we put into La Spezia.
There was a letter there from Uncle Pietro Gilardino, saying he was coming to visit me. The next day he came out to
the ship. He looked the same as I remembered him, and I
was so glad to see him I couldn't keep still. I showed him all
over the ship, and he asked many, many questions about my
work. He seemed surprised when he heard how hard I had to
labor, and I was a little surprised that he was surprised, for
by then I was just about used to it. I didn't like it, but I was
used to it.

Before he left, he said I was to come to dinner at his hotel
in La Spezia that evening.

I went to Lavagnini to get permission. "So it's your uncle,
eh Piemonte?" he said. "Well, well, you must go, of course."

Then I thought of something, and my face fell. I was close
to tears.

"What's the matter?" he said.

"I haven't got shoes to wear," I told him.

"Wait, we'll fix that up," he said, and somewhere found a
pair of sneakers for me.

That evening I rowed in and appeared at my Uncle
Pietro's hotel right on the dot. A business associate of his
joined us in the dining room, and while he and my uncle
were talking, I got busy on a basket of rolls that had been
placed on the table. Don't forget, I had had no fresh bread
for a long time, and so it was only a matter of minutes before
the basket was altogether empty. My Uncle Pietro was watching me as though amused, and when he saw that I had finished the basket he called to the waiter to bring another one.
I finished that, too, and a third one, and then I ate every

scrap of the big dinner that had been ordered. By the time I had my coffee I was so full I could hardly talk, but for the first time since being in the hospital I had enough to eat.

After dinner my uncle looked at me and said, "How do you like it on that ship, Cencin?"

"I don't like it," I said.

"I've never seen such calloused hands on a boy," he said, shaking his head.

"I work very hard, as I told you," I said to him.

"It is no life for a boy who comes from a family like yours." He was looking thoughtful.

I didn't say anything. I thought he was going to take me away with him, and I didn't want to do anything to cause him to change his mind. I wanted to get away from that ship too badly to risk it.

"Maybe," said Uncle Pietro, "I will send for you." That was all he would say. I was beside myself with hope. When I got back to the ship I could hardly sleep, I was so excited.

But, as usual, I was disappointed for a time. Days passed, and nothing happened. I found out later that Uncle Pietro had gone to my mother and urged her to send for me, and that she had written to Captain Lena, and he at first had refused. He did not like the idea of losing a deckhand who worked for nothing but meals. I was a great help to him by then, and boys were hard to get. But finally they persuaded him to let me go.

He called me into his cabin and said, "Here is money for your ticket back to Canelli, and a couple of extra lire to buy food on the train."

I grabbed the money, muttered something, and bolted out of the cabin. It took only a few minutes for me to gather together my things and to say good-by to Lavagnini and the crew members who had been decent to me. Then I was rowing away from the boat, my sailing days over for good.

The first thing I did when I got to La Spezia was to spend money for food. I went around buying bread, salami, and dried figs, stuffing them in my pockets until they were full. Finally I got on the train for Genoa. The next morning, when I got off, I found that I did not have enough money left to buy breakfast—or even to take the train from Genoa to Canelli. I had spent everything without thinking. I thought maybe I might be able to get on the train and talk the conductor into letting me ride to Canelli free, but then I found that the train was not scheduled to leave until noon, and it was still early in the morning. Broke and hungry, I started to wander around the city. As I was going along one narrow street, a miracle happened. There, to my astonished eyes, was my Uncle Gustavo. He and his family had moved to Genoa some time before—but of course I hadn't known about it. I waited until I was sure it was he, and then I ran up to him. He was surprised to see me, naturally, and he took me home and gave me some food and money. Then, at train time, he bought me a ticket and put me on the train, along with a business associate of his who happened to be going the same way. This man was very kind to me during the trip; he bought sandwiches and wine, and as we ate them he cracked jokes. All in all, it was a pleasant trip, but when I got to Canelli it was late at night, there were snow drifts on the ground, and nobody was there to meet me.

I waded through the snow to my father's house, so cold I was afraid I was going to freeze. My shirt was thin, and so were my shoes and pants. But as I got near the house, I knew something was wrong. I went up and knocked and rang, but nobody came. I went around the side and looked in one of the windows. The house was plainly deserted. I couldn't understand it; I was worried and frightened. I ran through the snow to my grandfather's house, where Uncle Pietro lived, but nobody came to the door there, either, when I rapped and rang. I gathered a few small stones and threw them up at one of the windows. After five minutes or so a light appeared and my oldest sister, Matilda, shaking with the cold, looked out and saw who it was. She came down and let me in and took me out to the kitchen, where she helped me get warm and cooked me some eggs.

"Where is the family?" I asked.

"They moved to Torino," my sister said.

"It's funny they didn't let me know," I said.

"You were always away at sea," my sister said. "Nobody knew how to reach you."

The next morning Uncle Pietro told me that our family had moved to Torino because the educational facilities were better there. My brothers and sisters were going to school and doing very well, he said. Then he added that he was going to engage a tutor to help me catch up on the lessons I had missed while I was a sailor. That morning he took me to the stores and outfitted me with a new suit and shoes, and shirts and a hat and an overcoat. In the afternoon he made arrangements to hire a tutor.

For a while it looked as though *Il Vagabondo* was going to settle down and learn to be a respectable gentleman, but as soon as I saw the tutor I had other ideas. He was a man who had always said, before, that I would never amount to anything. Now that he was being paid to teach me, he sang a different tune. He praised me to the skies to my uncle and grandfather. I didn't like that; it didn't seem right to me, somehow. But I studied as hard as I could, and for a while things went along fairly well. My Uncle Pietro treated me as he would have treated a son of his own. Each morning I would go to his room and get the keys to his business establishment, and then there would be a list of chores for me to do. Compared with the work I'd done on the boat, everything he asked was a cinch. When I was not studying, I made straight for Uncle Pietro's place and helped the workers in every way I could.

My friends were the sons of the cobbler, the carpenter, the blacksmith, the saddler, and the barber. We were in constant war with the sons of the doctor, the lawyer, and the wealthier businessmen. My aunts knew this, and it worried them. They thought I should associate with the elite of the town. I did not think so then, and I don't think so today; thank goodness, in this country we have no nobility. I have never had any respect for title and social position. But it was bound to cause some trouble at that time, this attitude of mine. I was always getting in fights with the boys of the so-called better class. This worried my aunts. They were convinced that *Il Vagabondo* had not changed.

Around that time someone put on a play in the town. The man who was to play the lead, the part of a lawyer, could not learn his lines. They gave me a try at the part, and I studied until I got it letter-perfect. On the night of the play, all my ruffian friends were in the audience. I walked on in clothes I had borrowed from my grandfather and my uncle, said my lines as they were written, and made a big hit. But the next day, when the tutor gave me an examination, I flunked. I had been so busy studying for the play I didn't have time for my lessons.

"Well, well, it's plain that the boy will never be any good," one of my aunts said.

"Yes, he will," said Uncle Pietro. "I have plans for him. Cencin, how would you like to go to England with me? I must go there on business."

I was very excited and wanted to get started right away. But first we went to Torino and said good-by to my parents. I found that I had all but lost touch with my family; I felt like a stranger with them. When I kissed my mother good-by, I felt a little sad, but not much. I suppose I had been away too long.

Now, in those days, to people around where I lived, crossing the English Channel was worse than crossing the ocean. I remember once that a cousin died in England, but nobody went to claim the body because nobody was willing to risk the crossing. My Uncle Pietro was no exception. We went to Paris for a few days on business, and I noticed that each day he became more nervous. As we neared Calais, his nervous-

ness increased. The fact is, he was scared stiff. Before we got
on the Channel boat, he prepared for the dread voyage by
getting three bottles of *grappa*. As soon as we were aboard
he found some companions and went into the smoking room,
and there, with the help of the *grappa*, he managed to get
through the trip. By the time we reached England I had to
help him get off the boat. Since I was used to the sea, I didn't
mind the trip at all. In fact, I enjoyed it. I roamed all over the
boat, exploring it. As we approached the coast, I went to the
bow and looked out, wondering what the future would
bring. Another new life was beginning for The Vagabond.

CHAPTER FOUR

London Days

BEFORE WE LEFT ITALY, my uncle had made arrangements
with a business associate to look after me while I lived
in England. A methodical, practical man, Uncle Pietro had
my future all laid out. First I was to learn English, and after
a year or two I was to go to Paris to live until I learned
French. Then I was to go to the French vineyard country to
learn more about the wine business. Since Uncle Pietro had
no son of his own, he planned that some day I would take
over his affairs. Meanwhile, I would travel about for him,
looking after things in places he did not care to go. Uncle
Pietro hated to travel.

Later in life I found out that it does not do to dislike
people on sight, but of course in those days I had not yet
discovered that bit of wisdom. Consequently, when I first
met Luigi, my uncle's associate, I felt immediately that I was
not going to be happy with him. I tried to get some of this
across to Uncle Pietro. "Nonsense, you'll be very well off
with him," he said. "Luigi is a fine fellow. He knows London well." When my uncle left, it was all I could do to keep
from breaking down.

Luigi had come from our part of the country at home. He
was a man of medium height, with huge black mustaches. He

made it plain from the beginning that he was not too pleased at having me as his charge. He was only doing it because he did not want to displease my uncle and lose his business. He had been in London many years and knew it as well as my uncle had said, but he made no attempt to communicate this knowledge to me. He seemed upset because I did not like to talk about women and drinking and carousing. He did not realize that this was because I was a boy; he thought there was something the matter with me. Soon he lost interest in me altogether. He grudgingly allowed me to share his rooms, but for the most part I was on my own.

Before long I struck up an acquaintance with a few Italian boys in the neighborhood. One of them told me I ought to get a job. When I relayed this suggestion to Luigi, he was delighted. "Fine, boy, fine," he said, and went back to drinking with his cronies. It was plain that he was glad to get rid of me, and for my part, I was pleased to get away from him.

The next morning, my friend took me to a woman who ran an employment agency, and she delivered me to a man and his wife who ran a boardinghouse near the rear of the British Museum. The man and woman were typically middle-class British, with sturdy, expressionless faces. They wanted no nonsense in their old, dark house; they made that plain right away. Since they couldn't speak Italian and I couldn't speak English, they simply led me to whatever jobs had to be done, pointed to the work, and pushed me into it. Believe me, there was plenty to do in that place. There were fourteen boarders living there.

When I arrived at the boardinghouse, the man first took me down into the damp, smelly basement and showed me where I was to sleep. It was a hard cot in a storage room. I could hear scuttling in the shadows, and I knew I would have company at night. Then, without a word, the man led me to an enormous tub of silverware and started me polishing it. That job occupied me until late in the afternoon. From time to time I had to interrupt it for another series of tasks which the landlord pointed out. He and his wife had four or five small mongrels which had the run of the place. None was housebroken.

Around six o'clock that evening the landlord gave me my first meal. It was a bowl of lukewarm haddock, left over from the boarders' table. There was a tiny sprig of parsley on it, for garnish. Also, there was a small cup of cold tea. "What, no bread?" I cried. He couldn't understand me; he shrugged his shoulders and walked away. All my life, like most Italians, I had regarded bread as an absolute necessity. If I had had some, the sad-looking fish might have been edible, since I was ravenously hungry. But there was no bread, and I couldn't eat. I threw the fish in one of the slop pails in the basement.

An hour or two later, the landlord came, took me by the shoulder, and pushed me into the yard behind the house. Then he locked the door. Somehow, I figured out that he and his wife were going out for the evening, and they didn't trust me in the house. Well, I thought, I'm not going to stay around here any longer; I'll run away. I started to climb the fence, but in the next yard were five or six ferocious dogs. I made sounds to try to quiet them down, but I guess the dogs didn't understand Italian, either. So there I was, stuck in that yard. It began to get cold. By the time the landlord came, took me back in the house, and pointed toward the basement, I was glad to go down and fall into my hard cot. I remember thinking as I fell asleep that the ship had been bad enough, but it hadn't been *that* bad.

The worst was yet to come. The landlord awakened me at six in the morning, took me upstairs, and showed me four-teen pairs of shoes—the boarders'. I had to polish them all. Then I had to help get breakfast and serve it, empty the slop pails, and wash the dishes. The food they gave me to eat that morning was a little better than the meal I'd had the night before: it was a plate of scraps the landlord's wife had culled from the boarders' plates. As soon as I was finished, they put me to making the beds. After that there was general house-cleaning. They kept me on the go all day long—and so did those terrible, unmannerly little dogs. Every time I finished cleaning up after one, another would get the same idea. I didn't get any lunch that day. Once or twice I went to the kitchen and told the landlady I was hungry, but again she couldn't understand what I was saying. She chased me out. A little later, when nobody was watching, I sneaked into the front hall and tried the door. It was locked securely. So there was no chance of running off by that exit. That evening I decided I would work a ruse on the landlord. I would tell him that my father was in London and that I wanted to go and see him; then, when I was outside, I would never go back. I went to the man and said, "Me Papa." He spread his hands to indicate that he couldn't make out my words. Then I remembered a phrase I had seen in Italy on products from England: "Patenta London." I thought it meant "in London." I said to the man, "Me Papa—Patenta London, Me Papa—Patenta London." He simply walked away. I don't know when I've spent a more miserable night. I felt so terrible, lying there in the dark on that hard cot, I didn't even pay any attention to the rats running around in the room.

The next day I had a plan. I wrapped up the few belongings I had brought and hid them in the darkened front hall. Then I rushed to finish making the beds, so I could get back downstairs. I began cleaning a room near the hall when the postman knocked. The landlord went to answer the door, and as he did I grabbed up my parcel, pushed past him, and ran out into the street. The landlord and the postman both took off after me, shouting and waving their arms, and for a time it looked as though they would catch up. It was lucky for me that I was younger and stronger and faster. Finally they gave up the chase. I ran on a few blocks, then sank down on the curb to catch my breath.

Thinking about what I would do, I finally concluded that I'd better try to get back to Luigi's house—even that would be better than the place I'd just been. I remembered the name of the street—it was near Soho Square and was called Manette. I went up to a bobby and tried to ask him how to get there, but again I couldn't make myself clear. I kept saying "Manette, Manette," over and over, and he began pointing first one way, then another. Finally I started out in one direction, but when I'd gone five or six blocks I found myself back on the same corner, with the same policeman. I asked him again, and again he pointed, and I started out once more. This time, when I found myself back on the corner, I was too embarrassed to ask him again. I kept walking until it began to get dark, and by then I was beginning to get scared. I thought that I might never get back to Luigi's, and that just because I couldn't speak English I might wander around London until I starved to death. Then, as I was passing by a pastry shop, to my joy I saw one of the Italian boys I'd met in Luigi's neighborhood. He spoke my language, of course. I'd never been so glad to see anyone in my life. He was washing windows in the shop, but he went inside and explained to the proprietor that I was lost and got permission to show me the way to Luigi's house.

When I got home, Luigi wasn't very glad to see me. I think he might even have beaten me if he hadn't feared that I might tell my uncle. "So you ran away, eh?" he said. "Well, tomorrow you get another job." That was all right with me; I didn't want to stay with him, and I didn't see how any job could be as bad as the one I'd just left. The next day he took me to a restaurant called the Victoria at the Notting Hill Gate.

There were four or five other boys working there, but I must say that even with the work apportioned among us, the place was not much better than the one I'd been in before. They set me to washing dishes at a sink so high that I had to stand on a beer case to reach it. When I was not busy with the dishes I had to peel potatoes and clean the slop buckets. We boys all slept together in a room above the restaurant, a garret with a low ceiling. It was hot, stuffy, and crowded.

Each evening, after we'd made the kitchen spick-and-span, the proprietor would take us upstairs with a candle. He would hold it for a few seconds while we undressed and got into our beds, and then he would leave. On the second or third day I innocently asked one of the boys why we had to go to bed each evening.

"Why can't we go out and have some fun?" I asked.

"Why, don't you know about Jack the Ripper?" he said, in surprise.

It is true that Jack the Ripper was abroad in those days. The proprietor used him as a threat to keep us in the garret. Whenever anyone ventured to ask to go out, the proprietor would say, "Well, all right, but if Jack the Ripper gets you, it won't be my fault." Naturally, everyone was too frightened to go abroad.

Each morning the proprietor would come in before daylight and awaken us by throwing water in our faces. Then would begin the work, which did not let up until after dark. We had only one form of amusement: we used to hunt rats in the basement of the place. Every time I tell about the rats in London in those days, people think I am exaggerating. They were as big as small dogs, and twice as fierce. We used to close everything up and go down in the dining room and basement and hunt them with clubs.

The only pay I received in the several months I worked there was in the form of food. Yet in spite of all the disadvantages, I found that I liked life in a restaurant. I looked enviously at the waiters, and thought of them as the aristocracy. The way to get to be a waiter, I decided, was to first become a cook. I began hanging around the cooks whenever I could, and by the time I left the place I had learned how to make an omelet, how to fry eggs, how to make sautéed potatoes, and several other things.

Then, one day, Luigi turned up. It was about three or four months after he had taken me there, and I suppose he

thought he'd better find out how I was doing, so he could
report to my uncle.

"How you like it here?" he asked.

"Not too bad, except the work is very hard," I said.

"How much they paying you?"

"Nothing."

"Nothing!"

"Nothing."

"This will not do," said Luigi.

"I want to leave and get better job," I said. "I can cook
a little. Maybe I can be kitchen helper in some other place."

Luigi went to the proprietor. "Give the boy his pay," he
said.

"Pay? What pay? His meals are his pay," said the proprietor. "And his lodging. He has nice room upstairs."

"Pay him," Luigi insisted.

"I pay him nothing," the man insisted.

Luigi called a policeman. There was a great row, with
much yelling and blustering. Finally the proprietor handed
over some money. I never found out how much it was, since
Luigi kept most of it himself.

With the small amount of money he gave me, I took a
room in a place near Notting Hill Gate, where some other
Italian boys lived. By that time I had begun to learn a little
English. I always listened carefully to what people said and
tried to imitate the sounds, and some kind souls in the
boardinghouse where I was staying took the trouble to give
me a few simple lessons. The hardest word for me to say, as
I recall, was "thunder." I could not seem to get it right; it
always came out "tunder," until the day when a fellow taught
me how to put my tongue between my teeth for the "th"
sound.

I devised a system for remembering English words. It went
this way: if I wanted to remember the word "horse," I would
think of the word in my native dialect which sounded like
it: *ors*. But *ors* meant bear, and so whenever I wanted to talk

about a horse, I would first think of a bear. For "boy" I would first remember *boier*, the word for hangman. Likewise, when I went to buy an overcoat, I thought of a cooked egg, or *ovacot*. It was a funny way to learn English, but it was a big help to me.

Soon after I took the room, I got a new job through an agency. I became a kind of houseboy to a family in Bayswater Road. The man was a civil engineer named Reed, with a beautiful wife of Spanish extraction, a son, and four daughters. They were very kind to me. After a while they asked me to live in, and they treated me like one of the family. There was a theatrical atmosphere in that household. The children were always doing recitations and acting out sketches, and Mrs. Reed had played piano in the concert halls. With their encouragement, I began going to night school. When I finally learned to read in English, I began going through the books in the Reeds' library. I remember that I particularly enjoyed Jules Verne's *Twenty Thousand Leagues Under the Sea* and some of his other books.

Mainly due to the Reeds' interest in the arts, I began going to the music halls and legitimate plays. Actually, I was more than mildly interested in the theater; I was stage-struck. The costumes, the gestures, the long, dramatic speeches fascinated me. One of the first plays I saw was *Sherlock Holmes*, at the Coronet Theatre, and I went back to see it again and again. Another I saw many times was *The Belle of New York*, which starred the famous Edna May, an American actress. She played the part of a Salvation Army lassie in that one, and I was reminded of it a few years ago when I saw Isabel Bigley as the lassie in *Guys and Dolls*. Later, when I was well established in my place in New York, Edna May came in for lunch. I thought how nice it would be to tell her that I had seen her years before—many years before—in London, and how much I had enjoyed her performance. I went up and told her, and she gave me a rather cool smile. It dawned on me that it is not exactly in good taste to remind a woman, and especially an actress, of her age.

Well, I began spending every spare moment and every penny I earned on the theater. One show I saw seven times. It was called *The Country Girl.* (I wonder if Clifford Odets knew about this when he wrote his play of the same name?) To tell the truth I liked the music halls a little better than the legitimate plays. I remember some of the stars—Vesta Victoria, Vesta Atille, Sir Harry Lauder, and a clown called Little Tich, who came onstage wearing a tremendous pair of shoes. Lauder was my favorite comic, as I remember. I used to try to imitate him to make my friends laugh. He would come on dressed as a schoolboy, pulling tops and marbles out of his pocket. He used to say that he couldn't go to school that day because his mother had lost the lid to a saucepan and he had to sit on it to make it boil.

One of the most stirring experiences I had was the time I went to hear John Philip Sousa's band, which had come over from America. I heard him in Queen's Hall, and I'll never forget the way that band played "The Stars and Stripes Forever." I remember telling a friend, "A country that can get up a band like that must be a pretty good one." I decided then and there that some time I would try to go to America.

Another passion of mine around that time was wrestling. My hero was Hackenschmidt, whom they called the Russian Lion. I used to watch everything Hackenschmidt did, and read everything that was written about him, and I started to go to a gymnasium to take wrestling lessons. The proprietor was a huge man named Sandor. He wore large neat mustaches, and I grew a pair of my own in imitation.

When I went to Covent Garden for the first time to see the opera, I forgot all about music halls, the legitimate stage, and wrestling. I was so excited by the first performance that I resolved that I would never waste my money on any other form of entertainment. Oh, the singers they had in those days! Madame Melba, Tamagno, and of course, the greatest

of them all, Enrico Caruso, whom I later got to know when
I worked as a captain at the old Knickerbocker Hotel in New
York. I couldn't afford to go to the opera as often as I
wanted to; so, in order to satisfy this desire, I got a job as a
claqueuer. Members of the *claque* were hired by performers
to burst forth with loud applause at appropriate moments.
I enjoyed the work as well as any job I ever had in my life;
I was paid only a few shillings, but I got a free ticket to every
performance.

Once the great Eleanora Duse came to town. Everybody
had been raving about her, and the papers were full of
stories about her, so I thought I would go and see what the
fuss was all about. I stood in line all night waiting for a
ticket (La Duse had no need of a *claque*). I remember that I
was impressed, but to this day I can't remember the name of
her play.

I remained with the Reed family about a year and then,
wishing to take a situation in the country, I went to work for
a family in a place called Bishop's Waltham, near Southampton. The people had no children, and I was quartered with
the gardener, cook, and scullery maid. They taught me more
English, and I kept my reading up to date. One week end a
cousin of mine from Italy, a steward on a Cunard liner, came
into Southampton and I went down to see him. He urged me
to get a job with a Cunard ship. "The pay is good, the tips
are wonderful," he said. My one experience with a ship had
been enough for me. "No, thank you," I said. Some years
later, by the way, this cousin wrote me that he was retiring
from the sea. "One more trip," he wrote, "and I will be
finished." The words were truer than he intended them to be.
The boat he shipped on was the *Titanic*.

One day in Southampton I heard of an opening in a small
Italian restaurant. I had already decided to become a waiter,
as I have said, and I applied for the job and worked for several months. Now in those days, waiters in the better restaurants were gentlemen. They dressed well, in tailcoats and

derbies and striped pants, and they swung canes as they walked to work. They wore flowers in their lapels. They were well trained for their profession, and it was an honorable one. Many of them were on equal social terms with their customers, and several I knew were very wealthy. Today, of course, in this country, it is all changed. Waiters see no dignity in their jobs. They become waiters because they can find nothing better to do, and usually they are just waiting for a chance to do something else. Consequently, they don't bother to really learn their calling as they should. I well remember what happened when Cino came to me and said, "Dad, I've decided I'd like to carry on the business."

"What about college?" I said. He was then studying at Columbia.

"It doesn't appeal to me. I'd rather be a restaurant man."

His mother was outraged. "Do you think we raised you to be a restaurant owner?" she demanded. "You've been to college—you should be a professional man."

I said, "There is nothing disgraceful about being a restaurant owner if you are well trained and do it right. Are you serious about it, Cino?"

He said he was, and I decided to put him to the test. First I sent him to the Ritz, to work under one of the greatest chefs in America, Louis Diat. He spent two years there in the kitchen, learning everything. Then later I allowed him to be a bus boy in our place, then a waiter, then a captain, and finally head waiter. Meanwhile he had to study the business end; he had to learn all about buying produce, making analyses of costs, etc. Finally, after about five years, I thought he was ready to take over the place. You see, the name Sardi meant something to people. It meant good food, excellent service, and a place where you could enjoy your dinner in pleasant companionship. I had worked hard to build up that reputation. I did not want to see it ruined by a boy with good intentions and ambition, but no knowledge of the business. I must say that Cino impressed me with the way he

went through the apprenticeship. When I was ready to retire, I knew that the place was in good hands. I think it is
to his credit that no one has ever come up to me and said,
"Mr. Sardi, it's not as it was when you were at the door."
That wouldn't be true. If anything, it's better. Of course, I
may be a little prejudiced.

But to go back to my story. I soon found that I wasn't
learning enough about being a waiter, a fine waiter, in the
Southampton place. I need to know more about how a gentleman behaves and lives, I thought. I went back to London
and took another job as valet-houseboy, and it turned out
to be the best decision I could have made. I went in the
service of Dr. George Newton Pitt, one of the best-known
surgeons in the Empire. Dr. Pitt was one of the chiefs in
residence at Guy's Hospital, and was a personal consultant
to the Prince of Wales, later King Edward VII. His house
was at 15 Portland Place, diagonally across from the palace
of the Duke of Battenberg, and directly opposite the home
of the Lord Mayor of London.

During those days I frequently saw Queen Victoria out
riding in her carriage. She was very old—her face was drawn
and wrinkled—but she always nodded to the crowds and sometimes gave them a feeble wave of her hand. I heard it said
that she was so weak they had rigged up an apparatus that
helped her nod her head.

Dr. Pitt had calls all over Britain. He went to Ireland,
Scotland, and the Channel Islands, and on some of the trips
he took me along. My duties were simple. I made appointments, went to fetch books from the library, received the
patients, and kept the office and consultant rooms clean. This
was the time of the Boer War, and for a while I was tempted
to join up—not because the military life appealed to me, but
because I saw in it a chance to make a small fortune. Several
of the Italian boys I knew had joined and gone to Transvaal
with trunks of old clothes, which they traded to the natives
at a great profit. After I talked it over with Dr. Pitt, I changed

my mind. I liked working for him. I was learning more English, so much so that when he asked me to teach his three children some Italian, I discovered that I had forgotten many of the words.

Around that time I had my first romantic experience, although to tell the truth it was not a very memorable one. Through my friends who worked in restaurants, cafés, and hotels I had met several girls. I walked out with one or two of them a few times, and one day I was surprised to get a note from a girl who was working as housemaid next door. It said, "There's better fish in the sea." The note surprised me because although I'd seen the girl around and thought she was pretty, I'd never known she was interested in me. The next day I went to ask her to go out, but she would have nothing to do with me. I was even more surprised and puzzled. Then one of my friends told me that she had several older brothers who told her they would punish her if she ever went out with "that Italian." That was the first time I'd ever had an incident of that kind happen to me, and it was not the last. But it did not happen too often. I had learned to pronounce the English language so like the English did that I managed to lose my foreign accent. In fact, most people thought I was an Englishman.

When I finally left Dr. Pitt, I felt that I knew enough about manners and customs to take a job as a waiter. The first situation I applied for, I was hired. I worked all over London in first-class restaurants and hotels—the Savoy, the Criterion, the St. James, and the Carlton. I achieved my ambition. When I went to work, I carried a stick and wore a flower in my lapel. Those were happy days. I took out pretty girls, I went frequently to the music halls, the legitimate theater, and the opera; I had plenty of money. I had learned how to be a gentleman. I was not yet twenty-one, but I thought of myself as a genuine man of the world.

Many years later I was telling some of my boyhood experiences in London to my son. "Why, Dad," he said, "that sounds like something out of Dickens."

"I don't know about that," I said. "But I do know that in those early days, I certainly had a dickens of a time!"

CHAPTER FIVE

Interlude in the Army

IT WAS JUST BEFORE DAYBREAK, and all around me in the darkness the men were making sputtering, coughing noises, waking up with difficulty, voicing good-natured complaints. Soon the light appeared at one end of the room, and the man came in with the coffee. I sat up in my bed, reached around and took my tin cup off the shelf, and waited for him to get to me.

If this sounds like life in some men's club, let the reader be set straight immediately. It was no club. It was the Italian army, during the time I was a conscripted soldier. During World War II, I used to tell some of my soldier customers how in my day the Italian soldiers got coffee in bed in the mornings. They would stare at me, then look at each other as if to say, Well, old Sardi's mind is beginning to go. But it was the truth. It was also the truth that I had a pretty good time in the army, all things considered. I had never expected to. When I first heard that the army wanted me, I was convinced that my happy days were at an end.

The fact is, I might still be a waiter in London today, swinging my cane on the way to work, if it had not been for the army. I might never even have come to America at all.

[71]

And so, what at first seemed like a disaster turned out to be a good break.

The good days in London had swelled my head a little, I guess. For one thing, Uncle Pietro had wanted me to move on to France to learn the wine business so I could take over his business. He kept urging me to make the change, and I kept ignoring his letters. Finally I wrote him and said I planned to stay in London. I never heard from him again as long as I was in London. He later got married, and I sometimes heard from his wife, whom I'd never seen, but Uncle Pietro was too proud to write. He felt that I had disappointed him. I was just young enough and headstrong enough to forget all the kind things he had done for me.

From time to time, my uncle's wife mentioned the conscription. So did my mother's letters. As time wore on, my mother sounded more and more worried. They wanted me to go in the service, she said, and she was afraid that if I didn't go home and serve my stretch they would come and get me and punish me. I thought that if I just ignored the letters they might forget me.

But one night I went out and had some drinks and dinner with a couple of friends who also had come originally from Italy. They, too, were wanted in the draft, and they didn't like the idea any better than I did. But as the evening wore on, and we had more drinks, we began reminiscing about the old country and the good times we'd had there.

"After all," one of my friends said, "it would be nice to go home again for a while."

I agreed. "And," I said, "everybody has to go in the service—it's not fair to the others who go to duck it."

We had some more drinks and talked some more. Finally we decided that the three of us would all quit our jobs, go back together, and go as we were called. We shook hands, and next day made arrangements to go.

I do not remember too much of that trip, except that we had a very good time. It was a little like Uncle Pietro's

voyage across the Channel the time he'd taken me to England—except that he was frightened, and we were frightened
only of running out of spirits. I do remember that once, on
the way, I realized how much I was looking forward to seeing
my home again. In the early days in London I had been
homesick, but gradually I had come to think of that city as
home. Whole weeks had passed in which I had scarcely given
my native land a thought.

When I reached Torino, I was disappointed. I found that
my family had moved back to Canelli to live. It was after
dark when I got to Canelli, and there was no sign of life in
my grandfather's old house. I went to Uncle Pietro's, but that
too was dark. Well, I thought, this is a fine welcome—but
then I realized that I couldn't really blame them, since I
hadn't told anyone I was coming. I started to wander aim-
lessly around the streets, wondering where they all might
have gone, when suddenly a horse and carriage clattered
toward me.

I recognized the driver immediately; he was one of Uncle
Pietro's men. "Ho, wait!" I cried.

A man in the coach stuck his head out. "What's the delay?"

"Domenico!" I cried. "Brother Domenico!"

"Cencin!" he yelled, hopping down. Then we were beating each other on the back and laughing and asking questions so fast neither could understand what the other was
saying. As I have said before, Domenico was an actor. He
had been playing either in Milano or Genoa, and he had
come home for the celebration—for this was carnival time.

"How surprised they'll be!" he cried. "What fun to have
you back!" Everyone, he added, was having dinner at our
father's old house.

"Let's play a joke," I said. "When we go up to the house,
I'll wait outside. You go in first, and tell them you're late
for dinner because you've been arranging a treat. Then I'll
ring the bell, and you open the door and pretend that I'm a

stranger. I'll go right by you and come in and surprise them all."

Domenico said, "Fine, fine," and we proceeded in my uncle's carriage up the hill to the house. I waited while he went inside, and as I stood by the door I could hear them calling him down for being late for the dinner. Domenico was never much good at keeping secrets; soon I could hear them saying, "He's got something up his sleeve—he's been up to some joke!" When I heard that, I rang the bell.

"Here," said Domenico, opening the door, "who are you? What do you want? Why are you here?"

I went right by him and into the room, where they were all sitting around the table. None of them recognized me—I was dressed in my London clothes, wearing a derby hat, a blue double-breasted suit, carrying a cane. The boy who had gone away years before had never dressed like that.

It was my Uncle Pietro's wife, the one who'd never seen me, who guessed. "Why, it's Cencin!" she cried, and then there was a repetition, on a bigger scale, of the reunion scene I'd had with Domenico. My mother and father and all the others were crowding around, and everybody was laughing and crying and exclaiming, and only my little grandmother remained at the table. She was so moved she could not even cry. She sat with a solemn face, pointing at the picture of my grandfather on the wall. Now, as a man, I resembled him, and the old lady was overcome.

Well, it was a wonderful homecoming. But the best part of it for me was when Uncle Pietro, who had been angry and disappointed, came up to me, threw his arms around me, and started to cry. Naturally, I followed suit.

During the days that followed, I found that my years in London had changed me more than I had thought. For one thing, I thought there was something peculiar about my family's way of talking. Italians use a great many gestures when they speak, and exaggerated expressions of the face. The quiet, reserved Britishers I'd been familiar with had never spoken that way. Without being conscious of it, I had adopted the English manner. So my family thought I was peculiar, too. Once, while the whole family was at the table, having some small discussion with everybody talking at once, I joined in. Soon I, too, was talking as excitedly as everybody else. But when I went to explain something to my mother, she burst out, "For God's sake, Cencin, move your hands! I can't stand it any longer!"

I spent some time wandering around the village and the surrounding countryside, revisiting old spots I'd known as a boy. I was conscious of a strangeness in my feeling about the place; it was as though I had never lived there at all. I was not homesick for London, because I had resolved that I would not think about the life I left behind. But somehow, although everything looked just about the same, I felt a restlessness. I remembered how I had been called *Il Vagabondo,* and I thought, maybe they were right. Maybe I will always be restless, everywhere, never satisfied with the old scenes and the old memories. Maybe I am meant to be a vagabond. I am still that way, I suppose. Most of us never outgrow the strong feelings we had when we were young. I remember how, when I retired from the restaurant, all I could think of was that now my wife and I were free to travel, to wander about, to see new things we had never seen before.

Presently it was time to go. When I said good-by to my mother and father, to my grandmother and Uncle Pietro and all the relatives, I somehow knew for certain that I might never see most of them again. I also knew I would never be coming back to Canelli to live.

When I had picked up my conscription papers at the city hall, I had found to my surprise that they had appointed me leader of the contingent from my commune. There were about seventy-five of us going off, and we were to report to the officer in charge of the military district at Casale. I was given the list of draftees to put in my pocket and warned not to lose it. The trip was without incident until we arrived at Casale. Then our plans were somewhat disrupted.

A few boys from Canelli and the surrounding area were waiting to welcome us. They were standing in the station, loaded with supplies. "Come with us," they said, "we are having a big farewell party for you."

"What about reporting with my list?" I said.

"Never mind that," they said.

"But it's the army," I said. "I understand they are very strict in the army."

"Look," they said, "we have brought *barbera* (red wine) and we are going to make *bagna cauda,* and we have brought oil and anchovies and salami and pimientoes and—"

"We can report later, I guess," I said.

So I went off with them, with the list still in my pocket. Some of the boys in the contingent found their way to the military headquarters without their leader.

The party lasted two days. To tell the truth, I do not remember much more about it than I did about the trip across the Channel coming back to Italy. It must have been a good one if it lasted that long.

The officers in charge were not too delighted to see us when we reported in. Even when I turned over the list they were not pleased. In fact, they threw us in the brig. We were sitting there wondering what was going to happen to us when along came a man whose face looked familiar.

"Say," he said, "are you Cencin Sardi?"

Wondering what my punishment was going to be, I nodded glumly. "I know your Uncle Pietro," he said. "Wait —I'll be back."

Soon we were released. It turned out that he had interceded for us with the officers in charge. We got off with a stiff reprimand. Not only that, but we had another unexpected break. Our names had been on the list to go to the horse-drawn artillery, but while we had been celebrating, that quota had been filled. Now we were to go to the infantry.

Meanwhile, there would be a week to wait around Casale. Our new officer friend arranged for us to go home for that week. I don't remember much of that furlough, either.

When I reported back, I learned that I was to be sent to Belluno, up near the Austrian border. By that time, having enjoyed my service in the army to date, I had resolved that as long as I was in, I was going to have a good time of it. The trip to Belluno was something of a celebration. I still had a bit of money left from England, some pounds sterling, and my friends and I made the acquaintance of some non-commissioned officers who were very glad to tell us all about army life while I was spending my money. Whenever the train stopped we got some wine and food. The whole journey was one long feast.

I did not like the many restrictions the army imposed, but I had resolved to make the best of it. Soon after I had had my early training, one of my friends who had come with me from London told me there was a job open in the officers' mess. He was already working there. I applied for the job, and they gave it to me instantly. From then on I had a fine time. I was familiar with the work, and it meant extra pay. It meant so much extra pay, in fact, that I didn't need my army pay, which was only a few cents a week. I gave that to a big Sicilian farm boy named D'Alessandro. In return, he shined my shoes and cleaned my rifle and kept my clothes in order. He also acted as bodyguard—and a man never had a better protector. If anybody ever made so much as a move toward me, this big fellow would swarm all over him.

Now that I look back upon my army days, there was only one hardship. It was very cold in Belluno. The snow was often several feet deep in winter. That coffee in bed each morning was very welcome.

For one week of every year there was a big celebration in Belluno, as there was in every other Italian town. The climax of this carnival was a fancy-dress masquerade ball. There was one officer in our regiment who fancied himself a great ladies' man. He was always boasting of his conquests in the mess. So, on the night of the masquerade, one of my friends dressed as a woman. He was very convincing—so much so that the lady-killer went after him immediately. All evening long, the "lady" flirted with him. The officer was beside himself with curiosity. Just before the masques were to be removed, our friend vanished out a side entrance. The officer was downcast. He kept raving to his friends about how beautiful the girl had been. He had some wine and declared that he would find her if he had to search to the ends of the earth. The next day, in the mess, some of us kidded him about the lady. We kidded him until he caught on. At first he was furious, but then he relaxed and laughed as hard as we did.

That ball, if I am not mistaken, occurred during my second year of service. During the celebration I spent so much money that I was flat broke. Finally I determined to write home to my father for some cash. This was the first time in my life I had ever asked him for money, and I did not want him to think I had been improvident. I told him I had lost my bayonet and had to buy a new one. His letter came almost by return mail. "Isn't that funny," he wrote, "when I was in the army, the same thing happened to me." I never forgot that gentle reprimand. It was the last time I asked him for cash, and from then on I was more careful with the money I earned. An English friend of mine, Stanley Begalow, had begun sending me the *People* every week, and that turned out to be an unexpected source of income. The officers were studying English, and when they heard that I had an English newspaper they asked me to help them with their lessons. Also, a lieutenant colonel hired me to tutor his daughter, a very attractive girl. Later I became a part-time interpreter, in the evenings, for tourists who were staying at the winter-resort hotels near the army installation.

As soldiers always do, we used to sit around in the evenings and talk about what we planned to do when our service

would be over. Several of my friends announced that they
were going to the United States. I had planned to go back to
London and become a waiter again, but the more I heard
them talking, the more attractive the United States sounded
to me. The way everyone talked, that was the only country
to go where the opportunity was equal and where a man
could make a fine living.

When I was released from the army, they wanted me to
re-enlist. They even shoved a paper at me. "My God," I said,
"isn't two years enough?" Believe me, I got away from them
fast!

As soon as I got back to Canelli I made arrangements to
get my papers and passport to go to America. One day, when
I came back from this task, my mother took me aside and
said, "Cencin, I want you to do me a favor."

"Anything," I said.

"I want you to take Eduardo with you and look after him,"
she said.

I hesitated. I was twenty-two years old, and a man that
age does not want a responsibility. My brother Eduardo had
never been out of Italy. He had tried to learn the wine business, but he had not been interested in it. My mother hoped
I would help him get started in something he liked. Seeing
the way she was looking at me, I agreed. I promised I would
look after him as long as I was alive, and I never broke that
promise.

There was one promise I did break, but I am not sorry
about that one. One night my aunt gave us a farewell dinner.
As it was over, I folded my napkin and laid it beside my
plate. "Three years from now," I said, "I will come back
from America and unfold it." At the time I meant it sin-
cerely. I planned to go to the United States, make a little
money, then go somewhere else and invest it in a business of
my own. As it happened, it was many more years before I was
to return. I broke the promise because I met my Jenny—
but that part of the story comes later.

In those days it was easier for an Italian to get into the United States than it is now. The quotas were not as restricted. I had saved a little money from the army, and I was well stocked with tobacco when I was ready for the voyage. (My brother smoked it all.) I figured that I had enough money to last me several months, in case I did not get a job at first. The boat we took on the crossing was a German ship, the *Batavia*. I believe it was the slowest boat in history; it took twenty-two days for the crossing from Naples to New York. But in reality it was a pleasant voyage. There were four other passengers, young fellows I'd known in my regiment, and we formed a convivial group. After the third or fourth day, we taught the German crew to cook Italian style. There were several pleasant young ladies aboard, and we had a good time with them. There was one part of the trip I will remember until the day I die. It was the morning we steamed into New York harbor and saw the Statue of Liberty. I cannot describe my feelings. I stood on the deck with the other passengers, most of us emigrants from lands across the sea, looking for the opportunity that America offered, and we all cheered. I felt, at that moment, that the most important part of my life had begun. The date was November 21, 1907.

CHAPTER SIX

First Years in America

NOW I HAVE TO SAY AGAIN that I wish I had kept a diary. This chapter, I admit, is going to be mixed up, because I have so many memories of the things that happened between the time I got to America and the time the first Sardi's restaurant opened. I suppose I could sit down and try to straighten out all the time sequence and put everything in order, but to be frank, I have too much fishing to do. And I have to play with my grandchildren.

One thing I am going to do: I am going to pull out the most important happening, my meeting with my wife, and give it a separate section by itself. That part comes next. Meanwhile, here are some things that happened before and atfer that memorable event, which occurred at the Bartholdi Inn.

The first night my brother and I arrived in America, we slept in a midtown Mills Hotel in a room that cost us thirty-five cents. It was not too bad, but it wasn't the kind of place we wanted to stay in for any length of time, so the very next morning we began looking around for a couple of rooms. One of us had the address of a waiter who was living in a boardinghouse on 39th Street between Eighth and Ninth avenues. We went over there and talked to the landlady, a

Mrs. Finney. She was a big woman—she weighed nearly three hundred pounds—and she was as kind as she was huge. She showed us the rooms, and we decided to move right in. I stayed with her practically until the day I got married. She didn't make her entire living from the boardinghouse business; she was also a pastry cook in hotels, and unless I am mistaken she would lease the houses and then sublet the rooms. Consequently, she used to move around every once in a while. Some nights I would get home from my job and find that she had moved. There would be a note on the door, telling me where to go to find my belongings and a bed to sleep in. She was very good to my brother and me; she treated us as members of her family. She made me open my first savings account in the American Savings Bank, on 42nd Street. I watched that bank grow from a little one-room operation into the great institution it is today. In later years, the president and other officers used to eat lunch in our place, which always made me feel good; it made me feel that I was helping them the way they had helped me.

After I got married, I lost touch with Mrs. Finney. I used to see her now and then, but after a while she moved again and then I didn't see her at all. I had word of her, though, and knew she had kept in touch with me. For a long time we had a mounted policeman who was a good friend; he was on duty every evening and on matinee days outside our place, handling the theater crowds. Everybody called him Lock-'em-up Riley. Back in the days when I lived with Mrs. Finney, he had been a bartender in a saloon on 39th Street, and he had known her, too. He told me that one day she came over to 44th Street and stood in front of my place, peeped inside, and then turned to him and said, "My, isn't that wonderful!" I often wish I had seen her again. She was a grand person.

Now, in those first few months I was in New York, the city gave me the blues. It was shocking to me. London had existed in my mind as the ideal large city, but London as I remembered it was nothing like this place. It was not such a mixture. In New York, it seemed to me, everything was mixed up. There were different kinds of buildings everywhere. People were always putting up and tearing down buildings. They were always digging in the streets and filling in the holes. The Ninth and Sixth Avenue Elevateds were running then, and I thought I had never seen anything so ugly. The streets under them were drab and dark, and the storefronts were covered with soot and grime. I thought to myself, When are they ever going to finish this city? Sometimes the noise really got on my nerves. Everything was shaking. I remember one time my wife and I had an apartment on West 39th Street next to a printing plant. In the evenings, when the big presses were running, our whole building would shake and tremble as though we were caught in an earthquake. When you went to bed, it was like being rocked in a cradle. One night a friend of ours, Peter Vercesi, also in the restaurant business (he later was in charge of banquets at the Biltmore Hotel), came to stay with us in a spare room. Before I went to bed, I looked in on him to see if he was comfortable. He was sitting on the edge of the bed, looking queer.

"What's the matter, Peter?" I asked.

"I don't know. I feel sick."

"What's wrong?"

He shook his head hopelessly. "I don't know. Everything moves."

I pretended to sympathize with him at first, but then I could not keep the joke any longer. I took him out in the kitchen and showed him the cups on their hooks, rocking as the building shook. (And that reminds me of another story about Peter. After years at the Biltmore, he finally retired because he could no longer stand the cranky, cantankerous customers. He retired to the country, bought a farm and a lot of horses and cows. Every last one was named after some customer who had given him trouble.)

I said that this chapter was going to be jumbled up, and

here is proof. I remember another reason I was nervous and
not too fond of New York in those early years. In that neighborhood around 39th Street, somebody was always getting
robbed. It is hard to believe today that robbers could have
been so bold, but it is true that they were so daring they
would back a truck up to your house and haul away all your
furniture while you were out of an evening. My wife and I
were always worried. When we finally moved away from
there, we rented it to our friend John Brasi, who later became our manager in the restaurant when it moved to its
second location. Brasi was then chief bus boy in the restaurant on the top floor of Lord and Taylor's department
store. He had come from a town near Milano called Brescia,
and he had decided to come to this country at the urging of
our good friend Mario Cremona, about whom I will tell more
later. Before coming to work for us in the restaurant he was
in Palm Beach, Florida, as manager of a club in which
Florenz Ziegfeld had a show called "Palm Beach Nights."
Later he had worked at the Ambassador Hotel in Atlantic
City, and in New York at the Vanderbilt and the Plaza. But
back in those early days he was chief bus boy. When we
moved out of that 39th Street place, Brasi decided to take it
over. One day he was sweeping the floor and heard a noise
behind him. There was a burglar, coming in the window.
Brasi has always been very good in an emergency. He was
good in this one, all right. He picked up the broom and
knocked the thug half out of the window!

Going back to my reactions to New York, I found after a
time that I was getting used to the changes and the city noise.
Now, after nearly fifty years, I am so used to the city that
I can't stay away more than three months at a time! It is
truly my home.

One of the first jobs I had in this country was at the restaurant of Louis Sherry, at 44th Street and Fifth Avenue, in
the same building now occupied by the Guaranty Trust
Company of New York. The main dining room was truly

luxurious, with great high ceilings, beautiful paneling, and marble floors; and the service and food were in keeping. Charles Pierre, who later built the hotel that now bears his name, was a captain. I learned as much about fine service there as anywhere I ever worked, because everything had to be perfect. If a party of six or eight came in, immediately two bottles of champagne were placed in ice buckets at the table, and there was a captain, two waiters, and an assistant to take care of the party. Louis Sherry also had a place in Rhode Island, the Narragansett Pier Casino, located opposite Newport, the New York society resort, and I worked there for a while, taking care of yachtsmen, visiting poloists, and other very particular customers.

Now in London, as I have said, I had studied hard to master English, and I was proud of the fact that I did not have much of an accent. I understood English very well, I thought; but I soon learned that I did not understand English as it was spoken in America. I had been hired at Sherry's through a friend who recommended me, but after a few days on the job I found that the speech peculiarities of my customers were giving me some trouble. One of my first customers said, "I guess I'll have some oysters—and I guess I'll have some soup, and then I'll have the roast beef." I went and got his roast beef and began serving it. The next thing I knew, he had called the head waiter, Fred, to complain. Fred called me over.

"Why didn't you serve this gentleman his oysters and soup?" he demanded.

"I didn't realize he wanted them," I said, truthfully. "He said he *guessed* he would have oysters and soup—I thought he was guessing, not ordering."

Well, that was finally straightened out. With the help of friends, I began to catch on to the American ways of speaking. I also began to catch on to American living habits. Waiters I knew who worked at other places convinced me that I probably would be able to make more money if I worked at a less exclusive place. "The work may be harder, but there are more tips," one of them said. I decided to take their advice, and I had a variety of jobs around town. I worked in Bustanoby's, on 39th Street, where the piano player was a hard-working young fellow named Sigmund Romberg, who later made a great name for himself with his operettas; and I worked in the Café Martin, down on 14th Street. There, I remember, the celebrations were always very wild, for many wealthy and influential people went there. One New Year's Eve, I recall, one of the lady guests set her dress on fire and was seriously burned. Not all of my jobs were right in Manhattan. For a while I worked in a restaurant called Santa Lucia at Coney Island. The owners of the Santa Lucia were Southern Italians, and they wanted a Northern Italian to operate their place, which was how I got the job. I didn't stay too long there because the section was very tough. There were numerous gambling games around, and many restaurants of questionable reputation, one of which featured young men dressed up as women. I couldn't digest that stuff, and I was glad to leave there. As I recall, shortly after that I went to work at Reisenweber's in Brighton Beach, and later to Long Beach, where Vernon and Irene Castle danced in their Castle-by-the-Sea. Now all the names are coming back to me: I worked in Rector's, not the original one, established by George Rector, but one operated by his son; in Murray's, an Irish restaurant on 42nd Street between Seventh and Eighth avenues, where they had a room done by Stanford White, the architect who was killed by Harry K. Thaw in a quarrel over Evelyn Nesbit. In Murray's, a man named Sherry used to stage the shows. Madame Sherry, his wife, would come in riding a white horse, like Lady Godiva—but dressed a little more warmly!

There were three places I worked that I liked best, and they stand out most prominently as I look back over those days. The first one I recall was the Montmartre, a first-class café and supper club located on the roof of the Winter Garden Theatre. I took this job soon after our son was born; we already had our daughter Anna, and I thought I had better get out and make enough money to meet the increased obligations that children bring. So, while I was working at the Montmartre, I had three jobs. I served lunch in the Lord and Taylor restaurant, dinner at the Yale Club, and finally went to work the supper-time-to-closing shift at the Montmartre. It was hard work, and on top of it all, my wife and I were then living in the Bronx, far up at 1506 Northern Boulevard, a long trip downtown in those days. But thank God, He gave me my health and I was able to stand it.

The Shuberts owned the Montmartre, but it was managed by Clifford Fischer, one of the foremost hosts of the day. It was a very big place, and the only time that I recall its being filled to capacity was when Al Jolson came up from the theater downstairs, with the entire cast of the show and the band, and put on a late performance. He was then playing in *Sinbad the Sailor,* as I remember. One of the regular customers of the place was the fabulous Diamond Jim Brady. He would come in with two girls, sisters, and order an enormous dinner. While the girls ate in a dainty, ladylike way, Diamond Jim would toss off dozens of oysters and quarts of orange juice. Then he would settle down to eat his regular meal—and how he ate! I never saw anybody who ate so much, before or since. There was another habitué of the place, not exactly a customer, who almost lost Diamond Jim for us. He was a slick-haired, handsome young man who always came in without a cent in his pocket but looking like a million dollars, dressed in a tuxedo. He would approach ladies sitting at their tables and ask them to dance, and then he would honor them by sitting down and allowing them to buy him a drink. Those of us who worked there did not like him or his friends. We called them lounge lizards, and we always put them out whenever we caught them trying to cadge a drink. This one young man claimed that he had been a landscape gardener in Italy, near Rome, but I honestly believe he was not used to hard work. He and his pals were fond of sleeping all day long and only coming out into the world after sundown, like bats. At that time Joan Sawyer was dancing at the Montmartre. Something happened between her and her partner, and they separated. She picked this young man to be her new partner, and taught him to do the tango. After that there was not much we could do about keeping him out of the place; he acted as though he owned it. But Diamond Jim made him stop bothering the women customers. One night the young man asked one of Diamond Jim's lady friends to dance, and this so enraged the big man that he sent word that if he ever saw the young man in one of the places he patronized, that place would lose his patronage. Soon after that, the young man went to Hollywood. We never saw him again, but we heard of him. So did the rest of the world. His name was Rudolph Valentino. I remember how astonished I was when I saw him in *The Four Horsemen of the Apocalypse*.

The second favorite place was the old Knickerbocker Hotel, at 42nd and Broadway. This place, operated by James Regan, who formerly had been a bartender, was one of the best-run hotels in New York. Regan was a very tough fellow to work for, and to tell the truth I never heard much good about him, but I got along there all right. I was a captain in the café, and that was similar, in those days, to being a captain in Sardi's today. The Knickerbocker was one of the places where the theatrical people went for lunch—perhaps the most important place. Enrico Caruso lived at the Knickerbocker when he was in town, and he was king there, perhaps because Regan knew what a drawing card he was. Whenever Caruso was in the dining room, the place filled up. He pretended never to notice anybody, but just went about his business. Caruso was a Neapolitan, and very canny, very clever. There was always a sketch pad by his elbow, for he liked to make caricatures; whenever he sat down, he would take up the pad and begin to draw immediately. Every once in a while ladies would come over to him to tell him how much they enjoyed his voice, and he would always smile and pay compliments to them, but under his breath he would mutter. He had a good appetite, but his food always had to be prepared exactly the way he wanted it, and the waiter not only had to be good as a waiter, he had to be a good conversationalist too, witty and ready with a joke. For this kind of service, he tipped very well; and if he liked you, nobody could fire you, not even Regan. He used to walk across the lobby and begin talking to me before he was halfway to the door of the café, and we always had a conversation before he ordered. He told me how disgusted he was with the women who always tried to get a table near him in hope that he might draw their pictures; but to tell the truth, I don't believe he minded them at all. Like most Neapolitans, he was a flashy dresser, in loud, checked clothes and a lot of diamonds—he looked like a real Broadway sport of those days. He had a certain practical joke he always played. When a man and woman were sitting together, he would pretend to recognize the woman and go over to speak. The man, naturally, would stand up, and Caruso seemed to get a great kick out of keeping the poor man on his feet while he went on paying compliments to the lady.

Caruso's presence brought in other famous people of the opera. Giovanni Martinelli came in, I recall; he and I are now old friends. Gatti-Casazza was often in, too, and so were Didur, Melchior, Scotti, and Rothier. But the opera people actually were in the minority. The room was monopolized by famous people of the stage. George M. Cohan, the great Yankee Doodle man, used to lunch there almost every day with his old partner, Sam H. Harris, and A. H. Wood, another impresario of the day. Wood was one of the most liberal men I ever knew; he would pass out Corona Coronas by the handful. Sometimes there were just the three of them at that table, sometimes up to sixteen. It was in this place, too, that I first became acquainted with many other producers, composers, and other theatrical people: Morris Guest, Victor Herbert, Lee Shubert, and Samuel L. Rothafel, known as "Roxy." Julian Eltinge, the female impersonator, was often there for lunch. There was also a man who was looked upon with respect by some and with derision by others. His name was Marcus Loew. He had been a fur dealer, but after leaving that business he had started traveling around with a projector, renting empty storerooms and halls, showing motion pictures. He and Adolph Zukor became partners, along with David Belasco, another legendary showman. Around 1912 he brought in a movie the famous Sarah Bernhardt had made in France, *Queen Elizabeth,* and made a great deal of money with it. This was his first big success, I believe, and enabled him to begin setting up what later became a fantastic movie empire. There were other famous New Yorkers who used to linger over cigars and coffee in that café. There was a man who later became governor, Al Smith, who was always extremely kind and helpful to me, giving me advice whenever I asked for it; and my first meeting with Fiorello H. La Guardia occurred there, too. The heavyweight champion, Gentleman Jim Corbett, came in often. It was around that time that he left boxing for good and became an actor temporarily. He went into a play called *The Burglar and the Lady,* thereby prompting more than one critic to express the wish that he had remained in the ring. I stayed at the Knickerbocker a good long time, until the Hotel Biltmore opened; then most of the staff were offered good jobs over there, and when I saw all of them going, I decided to go, too. The man in charge at the Biltmore, Malnati, was one of the toughest men to work for in New York. At first I did not like the job. Then I realized that he knew his business as nobody else did. I learned as much from him as from anybody I ever knew.

Now I come to the best job I ever had in the most elegant and exclusive place I ever worked, the Palais Royale, owned by Paul Salvin, Jimmy Thompson, and, I think, a man named

York. There is nothing around these days like the Palais Royale, which was then located on 48th Street between Seventh Avenue and Broadway. What a place it was! Everything was first-rate—the food, the service, the shows, the decorations, and of course, the prices. It was in this place that John Murray Anderson first began producing the extravagant revues for which he later became famous. He always did things with a lavish hand, and I suppose he must have fallen into the habit at Salvin's place, for no expense was spared. The girls used to come down a huge staircase, dressed in costumes that looked as though they had been made for the harem of some Oriental emperor. Later, Anderson did *The Greenwich Village Follies* and many other shows; for years he was in charge of productions at Billy Rose's Diamond Horseshoe, and John Ringling North uses him today as designer of the spectacles for Ringling Brothers Circus—but I am certain that he has never done anything quite like those Palais Royale shows. It was a pleasure to work there just to watch them.

There were other pleasures, too, among them the heavy money. That was the place where I first began to pay income taxes to Uncle Sam. It often seemed to me that I was the only person among the service staff who paid the taxes, but I was proud to do it. I made a lot of money there. It was wartime—the United States had not yet gone into the war—and the merchant mariners and soldiers and sailors who were in port for one reason or another, and the visiting dignitaries from foreign countries all flocked to the Palais Royale. Most of them were big tippers and extra-heavy spenders. I had a system figured out, and by using it I managed to get a good share. The system was this: those of us who were captains used to take turns at different stations, for some were better than others. The one nearest the show floor was the best, the one back by the stage door was considered the worst. One day I told the *maître d'* that I would take the one near the stage door permanently. Everybody thought I was crazy. "You won't make any tips," they all said.

That was what they thought. I had become friendly with all the girls in the show. When they sat down to eat their evening meal, I always stood about and took care of their needs, joked with them, asked about their families, and got to know their names. You see, I had learned that the best customers always came to see the showgirls; they were the best customers, from a waiter's point of view, because they tried to impress the girls by spending a lot of money and tipping heavily. Because the girls and I were friendly, they always asked for me. That meant that the best customers in the house always wound up in my station. I worked then with a partner, my friend Joseph Bronzo. My, what a skillful man he was! He could bone a pheasant with two or three strokes of his knife. Bronzo did the carving, I did the talking. The tips rolled in. Soon the other captains caught onto this, and they began to squawk. The *maître d'* said, "You were pleased when Vincent took that station, because you thought he would make no money; now that he has built it up, it is his to keep."

I made many good friends at the Palais Royale. The girls in the chorus were good friends; occasionally they came to see my wife and me and the children in the afternoons. Another good friend was Franklin D'Amore, an acrobat, who worked with a partner named Charlie Douglas. When they first opened, they were afraid that they were not going to make a hit. I liked Frank, and I remembered my days in the *claque* in London; I had all the bus boys and the unoccupied waiters lined up, ready to give D'Amore and Douglas a big hand when they finished their act. They were a hit—our clapping started the audience, and as it turned out, the boys stayed in the show twenty-five or twenty-six weeks. Later, when my wife and I moved downtown from the Bronx, we had an extra room in our apartment, and we rented it to Frank. He was like one of our family; when he came down with the

Spanish flu, my wife nursed him until he was recovered. He later retired as an acrobat and went into business in California; I see him whenever he comes East. While I am speaking of that 56th Street apartment—I mentioned before that this chapter was going to be mixed up!—I remember some good friends of ours who lived across the court, a Mr. and Mrs. McCauley, whose son, Jack McCauley, later became a big star in musical comedy. He had one of the best parts in *High-Button Shoes,* a few seasons ago; that was Phil Silvers' first big Broadway hit, and also featured another Sardi regular, Nanette Fabray (who will be remembered for her parts as Baby Nanette in the original *Our Gang* movies).

There, I have wandered off again. The Palais Royale also was responsible for my meeting Paul Whiteman. He brought his band in from the West Coast, the original one, with such famous musicians as Henry Busse, the trumpet player, and Mike Pingatore, the banjoist. Later, when I opened my own place, they used to eat with my wife and me all the time— and they brought in other musicians and orchestra leaders.

Yes, those were happy days at the Palais Royale. The customers were as lavish with their money as the management was with its facilities. One man, a Russian, a railroad owner, I believe, used to be my favorite customer. When he came in with five people, he wanted five quarts of champagne immediately. When he tipped, he simply reached into his pocket and gave Bronzo and me a fistful of bills; sometimes it was $100 or more. Roy Wingate, the architect, was another good customer—but he never wanted to see the amount of the check. He paid a bill later and always told us to add whatever we thought was reasonable for the tip. He kept urging me to go into business for myself. As a matter of fact, that was exactly what was on my mind. Ever since I had come to America, it had been my ambition to have a place of my own. I did not have to wait too long. But before I tell about that, I must tell about how and where I met my Jenny.

CHAPTER SEVEN

The Bartholdi Inn

A ROUND THE TURN OF THE CENTURY, the Bartholdi Inn was the best-known theatrical hotel on Broadway. It was located right on the Great White Way, on the east side of the street at 45th, where Loew's State movie theater stands today. At first the Bartholdi consisted of a single, four-story brownstone house, with two tiny shops in the front on the ground floor, one belonging to a hairdresser and one to a woman who sold corsets. Later, as business got better, the owner of the Inn expanded it. She bought an adjoining house on 45th Street, and then another and another, and at the peak of her prosperity the Inn consisted of a row of seven houses, all linked together, running in a row. Many memories were made in that place; today, when the really old-time stage folks get together to talk about that period in show business, their conversation almost always gets around to their Bartholdi days.

In 1907, when I first went to work there, the Bartholdi Inn was already popular. After all, it was in a wonderful location, squarely in the center of the entertainment district. But its habitués were attracted by something more than the Inn's handiness. They went there mainly because of the personality of the lady who operated it, Mrs. Theresa Bartholdi. As long as I live, I will never forget this big-hearted lady and her kindness to my wife and me. Mrs. Bartholdi was a brunette whose shiny black hair perfectly set off her dark eyes. She was the sort of woman whom everybody called "Madame" automatically, out of respect, and yet although she had a fine business head, her good, generous nature was evident in everything she said and did. Compared to her, I was an amateur at extending credit to actors and actresses. She was always carrying several who were down and out and had no hope of working for some time. She was exceptionally patient, she never dunned, and she had a charming sense of humor about delinquent customers. A friend of mine remembers an actor named Johnny Powers, who owed her nearly $400. One night Powers invited a ball-player named Marty McHale to have dinner with him at the Bartholdi. After dinner and several pitchers of beer, the two men began to harmonize. Mrs. Bartholdi appeared in the doorway. She regarded them for a moment and shook her head. Finally she spoke to Powers. "How can you be so happy," she said, "and owe so much?" That was as close as she ever came to asking him for her money.

The rooms at the Bartholdi were never very expensive— and compared to prices today, they were amazingly cheap. You could get one of the better ones for $3 or $4 a week! My wife recalls that John Drew and Maurice Costello, whose rooms were among the very best, paid only about $11 or $12 a week for them. There was one section of the hotel where the rooms were cheaper—and perhaps a little darker—than the others. This was where actors used to go when they had fallen behind in their rent. They called it "The Lehigh Valley," and the phrase became a standing joke. It derived from the fact that the towns which were among the hardest to play —Scranton, Williamsport, Shamokin—were located in Pennsylvania's Lehigh Valley.

The food at the Bartholdi was inexpensive, too; there was a special steak sandwich that sold for a quarter. A friend of mine recalls that Sime Silverman, the founder of *Variety* (his office was just next to the Inn, on 45th Street), once urged Mrs. Bartholdi to take the special steak off the menu. "People who aren't in show business might find out about it," he said.

Cheapness aside, proximity to the theatrical district aside, stage people went to the Bartholdi because the place was more than a hotel. Mrs. Bartholdi actually gave her customers a kind of second home, and everyone was treated as part of the family (my wife and I remembered this when we opened our place, and I often think that it was one of the principal reasons we were successful). The dining room, situated on the first floor, was run like any other restaurant—that is, there was a menu and patrons had a fairly wide choice of food— but it resembled a private home in that the tables were big and round, and the guests sat with each other, laughing and joking, calling back and forth, as though they were all related. The dining room was such a warm, friendly place that it became a sort of hangout for actors who did not stay there, and even attracted people from other walks of life. For example, one of the regulars was Harry Hershfield, now famous as one of the panel members of the radio program, "Can You Top This?" as well as other shows. Harry lived there for a time, but even after he moved away he would still drop in nearly every night. In those days he made his living as a cartoonist, and he was a very successful one. He created two famous strips, "Desperate Desmond," and "Abe Kabibble" (the name of the latter was suggested to him by another Bartholdi custormer, Fanny Brice). In those days, Harry was noted for the tremendous store of jokes he carried around in his head. He always had a new one for the Bartholdi regulars; and today, as his radio appearances prove, he hasn't lost his touch. In fact, I understand that last year, just after the election, when President Eisenhower was planning his trip to Korea, he consulted Harry to get some stories to take over to tell the soldiers.

Harry would turn up in the dining room around eleven each night, sit down and chat with other Broadway people who had already congregated there. Presently, as curtains began going down in the area, others would drift in. Soon there would be quite a crowd; and after exchanging greetings, they would break up into groups and resume two marathon card games; one group played Chinese fan-tan, and the other played pinochle. Among the most popular of the card players was King Baggot, who later became nationally known as Mary Pickford's leading man. Baggot was a handsome fellow who had played in a large number of Broadway successes, including *Salomy Jane, Mrs. Wiggs of the Cabbage Patch, The Squaw Man,* and *The Bishop's Carriage.* After this long string of successes, he was persuaded by Harry Salter to make a film in which he appeared with Florence Lawrence. It was so successful that he left the stage for good, and in the days when he was around the Bartholdi he was making one movie every week. He was often accompanied by a friend of his, a cripple, who must have done him a good turn at some previous time. The man was bad-tempered and often abusive, but King took care of him as though he were a child, helping him downstairs, seating him in the dining room, and generally looking after him. When King was not living at the Bartholdi he still continued to take his evening meals in the dining room. He always pretended to be very worried over his losses at cards, which amounted to around twenty-five cents a night. One night, after losing a quarter, he left the game around midnight and never came back. None of us ever saw him again, in person. He had gone to Hollywood to stay. The person to whom he owed the quarter was Virginia Cowley, a leading lady in stock companies who stayed at the Bartholdi between seasons. For many years thereafter she wrote King a threatening letter on the first of each month, demanding her quarter. He always wrote back inviting her to come to Hollywood and collect it in person. I don't know if she ever accepted the invitation. More than that, I don't know what ever became of King; not long ago I heard that he was a bit player on contract to one of the big studios in Hollywood. But while he was at the peak of his popularity, he was a great personality. The Screen Club, formed in New York in 1909 by actors, producers, and directors in the new movie industry, honored him by electing him its first president. My wife still has among her souvenirs a booklet published at the time the Club gave a dinner for King. We were looking through it not long ago, and it was a little saddening for us to think of all the old organizations which are no longer in existence. Many of them—Imp Pictures, The Eclair Company, Ramo Films, The Lubin Company, The Edison Company—faded out before the industry really began to grow. But some of the individuals in the book are still going strong—Adolph Zukor, the producer, for instance. He used to come into the Bartholdi frequently. So did another famous Screen Club member who became a movie idol—John Bunny. Mary Pickford stayed there for a short time and so did Mack Sennett.

In those days the pioneer movie-makers were very active in studios at Fort Lee, New Jersey, and in various locations uptown in the Bronx. Many of the movie-makers stayed at the Bartholdi. Pearl White lived there, and so did the handsome John Gilbert and the equally handsome Wallace Beery, who in those days was playing romantic leads far removed from the rough, salty roles he had in later life. Thomas and Ralph Inch, Lotte Briscoe, Ralph Morgan, Bert Lytell, William S. Hart, and Hobart Bosworth, all of whom became famous in films, were constantly in and out of the place, and unless I am mistaken, Francis X. Bushman was, too.

When I first went to work at the Bartholdi, all the theatrical people were very much excited over the doings at Fort Lee. The card games were often interrupted by violent arguments over whether or not this new invention was a novelty or a lasting and important form of entertainment. There was one boarder who was positive that the future of the thespian world lay in the motion picture. He ate, drank, and slept movies. Although he was making shorter pictures, he had in mind a massive job, an epic. Sometimes, when the weather was bad and he and his crews couldn't work, and occasionally late at night when the card games had broken up, he and his actors would rehearse scenes for this forthcoming picture in the dining room, using tablecloths for costumes. He was a very dynamic man, and just by watching him I was sure that some day he would amount to something in the world. He was as passionate as a religious fanatic in his beliefs. One day, I asked one of the actors his name. "David Wark Griffith," he told me. Later I learned that the picture Griffith and his companions had been rehearsing was indeed an epic, one of the most important films of all time—*The Birth of a Nation.*

Not all the guests at the Bartholdi were as serious as Griffith. The Lee Brothers, I am reminded by my old friend Virginia Perry, who also stayed there, used to keep us in an uproar with their foolishness. One Lee had an important role in the great play *Everywoman,* and the other did what he called "Thomas Foolery" in several plays. I could never tell them apart, nor could most of the guests, for they were identical twins. They would always meet at the foot of the stairs after the evening performance and announce their arrival to the dining room crowd by pretending to stage a fight, shouting, "Stand back, you dog!" and "How dare you, sir!" They usually came in the dining room pulling each other's hair. One night Elmer Booth, who was appearing in Douglas Fairbanks, Sr.'s, show, *A Gentleman of Leisure,* said to one of the Lees, "I saw you at Jack's this afternoon with Miss B——." The girl in question was the friend of the other Lee, who promptly stood up, took off his coat, and challenged his brother to a fist fight. "Wait, wait," said Elmer, to the injured twin, "obviously, she took your brother for you." That seemed to satisfy him, and they sat down and resumed their card game.

I have another recollection of Elmer Booth. One night as he was eating, his boss, Douglas Fairbanks, appeared in the dining-room door, standing on his head.

"Elmer," said Fairbanks, "everything is upside down in the show and we've got to go over some scenes at ten A.M. Be there!" He turned a cartwheel and departed.

Few actors I have ever known have been able to stop acting off the stage. In fact, I have heard that after Loew's State was built, a comic said on the stage, "There were better actors in the old hotel on this site than will ever get on this stage.' They pulled him right off! Because there were so many actors, there was always a good deal of impromptu entertainment around the dining room. Nat Wills, the famous tramp comic of vaudeville, was in the place most of the time. So was Joe Yule, also a vaudevillian and today remembered mainly as the father of Mickey Rooney. Olive Briscoe, another headliner, was a steady boarder, and so was the team of Green and Keno—or was it Keno and Green?—who were the parents of Mitzi Green. When Irving Berlin wrote "Alexander's Ragtime Band," the Bartholdi crowd knew it word for word for weeks before it reached Broadway. Rita Redman, who introduced it, was a guest, and she sometimes got up during dinner and went through her entire repertory. Barney Bernard, of the original "Potash and Perlmutter" act, used to come in with his partner, Julius Tannen, and they sometimes ran through their routines for us. Lon Haskell, a burlesque comic, kept us in an uproar with his antics. There were also some brilliant conversationalists. Not long ago my wife and I were reminiscing with Eva Condon, an old friend of ours whom we met at the Inn. She reminded us of a conversation between Arnold Daly and Aubrey Boucicault, both actors, which was so remarkable that the card players stopped and everyone gathered around to listen. Miss Condon, incidentally, is a remarkable person herself. She holds the distinction of having appeared in three Pulitzer Prize Plays— *Icebound, Strange Interlude,* and *You Can't Take It with*

You. Today you can see her on television; she has made the change with the same grace she displayed when we knew her in the Bartholdi era.

As I have said, Mrs. Bartholdi and her daughters, Pauline and Edith, watched over all these people as though they were her own children. Drew Morton, a director, was one of Madame's favorites. He had done several Broadway shows, but his specialty was organizing high-class stock companies. Virginia Perry, in a recent letter, told me the sad story of his end: how he became desperately ill at the Inn and how Mrs. Bartholdi neglected her business to take care of him. When the doctor advised sending him to a hospital, he begged Mrs. Bartholdi not to send him away. She was forced to do so, however, and he died shortly after he reached the hospital. For a time, Mrs. Bartholdi was inconsolable—although it was not by any means her fault. She had given him the best possible care, but she blamed herself for his death.

The actors, in turn, sometimes watched over Mrs. Bartholdi. There were always a good many fires at the Inn, mainly due to the faulty wiring throughout the brownstones. There were so many, in fact, that it came to be a standard house joke that fire horses used to stop automatically whenever they passed by. At one fire alarm, a vaudevillian—I forget her name, but she was a strong woman—picked up her trunk and was prepared to hurl it out the window on the crowds in the street below. Someone stopped her just in time. Another time, one lady guest became so agitated over an alarm that she rushed down to the bottom of the stairs and sat there weeping, clad only in her nightgown and a big picture hat and clutching her bird cage. She never gave a thought to her money or jewels. Soon after I went to work there, a fire broke out which was worse than any we'd had before. The morning after, I had my first demonstration of the hearts of show people. Lined outside Mrs. Bartholdi's office were almost every one of the guests, waiting to give her money, jewels, valuables—whatever she needed, and none of them expecting anything in return.

I have often wondered what it is that makes theatrical people so generous, and the nearest I have ever come to an explanation is this: the stage is such a hard life, full of so many disappointments and breaks that never come, that it humanizes people. It makes them grateful for anything good that happens to them, and eager to help others. Pearl White first came to the Bartholdi because of her good heart. The well-known cliff-hanging serial heroine had been living in a rooming house down in the thirties. The hard-boiled landlady who owned that place had evicted a consumptive man who couldn't pay his rent, and Pearl was so angry that she left, too. Then she called a policeman, and the two of them searched that neighborhood until they found the sick man. She paid his rent and moved to the Bartholdi, and she often said that the reason she stayed was because Mrs. Bartholdi was the only landlady she knew who had a heart. There is a sad story with a happy ending, looking at it one way, connected with Pearl's stay at the Inn. Also living there was an actor named Ford Sterling, who fell in love with her on sight. Pearl, who was interested in the movies to the exclusion of everything else, gave him no encouragement. Poor Ford lost his appetite and couldn't work. On top of that, he took an unmerciful ragging from the other guests. Before many months he was deeply in debt to Mrs. Bartholdi, who never once dunned him or complained about his back rent. Finally he decided to leave New York for good and go to Hollywood. He did, and was an instantaneous hit as one of the original Keystone Cops. Pearl White's principal swain at the time was Harry Hershfield, but he says that he stopped going around with her when she began smoking big black cigars on the street!

Another Bartholdi romance, this one more flourishing, involved Robert Cummins, a tall, handsome, and very successful actor, who was well known on Broadway and seldom without a part. Bob had a good business head. With Mrs. Bartholdi's advice, he invested some of his savings in Long Island real estate and did very well. But he also had an impish, mischievous sense of humor. He took everything with a light heart, even his love life.

His lady in those days was Clara Campbell, who was as tall and beautiful as Bob was handsome. She worked for a fur coat manufacturer downtown as a model, and also lived at the Bartholdi—in a room on the first floor, down the hall from the dining room. Well, Clara was deeply in love with Bob and jealous to the point of being miserable most of the time. They often quarreled, and I am afraid I must report that some of the guests took advantage of the convenient location of her room to listen in on some of the more notable battles. After they had made up, Bob's sense of humor would come out and he would play a trick on her. One afternoon he waited until nobody was around and then, knowing that she had left her door unlocked, sneaked into her room and left a half-smoked cigar on a table near the door. He then waited for Clara to come home from work. At the bottom of the stairs, he greeted her with enthusiasm, kissing her, declaring his love. Arm in arm, they walked to her room. A second or two later he burst out with a cry of rage. He demanded to know who the man was, accused her of two-timing him with other men, and finally stalked out and was not seen for twenty-hour hours. After that, Clara was a little less jealous. Someone told me later that they were married and that it was a very happy union, but I lost touch with them after I left the Bartholdi.

I worked at Mrs. Bartholdi's, off and on, for nearly a year. In that time I was *maître d'*, captain, waiter, and bus boy all rolled into one. The work was hard, and I probably could have earned more money somewhere else. I stayed because I liked Mrs. Bartholdi and the people who lived at her place —and most important of all, because Mrs. Bartholdi's chief housekeeper was a lovely dark-haired, brown-eyed girl named

Eugenia Pallera. Now, ever since I was old enough to begin
thinking about girls, I'd had an eye for them, and I'd gone
around a lot. You might even say that I was something of a
sport. But when I saw this little girl in Mrs. Bartholdi's, I
forgot all the rest of them.

Eugenia came from Castel Alfero, in the same northern
Italian province as Canelli. She had come over in May, 1907,
with a cousin, and after staying with some relatives for a
time she had gone to work for Mrs. Bartholdi. At the time I
met her, she was living in the Bartholdis' residence down at
232 West 45th Street, where the Booth Theatre stands today.
Mr. Bartholdi was a semi-invalid. He and his wife and two
daughters, Pauline and Edith, made Eugenia feel like one of
the family, and I have always loved them for that. As Mrs.
Bartholdi became more and more occupied with business
matters outside the Inn, Eugenia was given more and more
to do. Before long she became a kind of general manager.

The first time I saw her, I knew that the Bartholdi was the
place for me to work. My wife remembers that it was at a
time when fresh peaches were in the markets. She happened
to mention that she liked peaches, and according to her, I
ran right out and bought a basket of them and presented it
to her, with a flourish. Everybody around the Inn called her
"Jenny," but in those days that was not descriptive enough
for me. I gave her a nickname of my own, *Cita,* meaning
"small one." She was tiny and delicate, and the prettiest
thing I'd ever seen.

I wish I could say that our courtship was a smooth one,
never marred by a spat or a disagreement. It was no such
thing. A pretty girl always has a lot of admirers, and since
Jenny was prettier than most girls, I had plenty of rivals. In
fact, the reason I worked at the Bartholdi off and on was
because I was so jealous of the competition. I would tell her
that she shouldn't see anybody else but me, and she would
tell me not to be silly, or words to that effect. Then I would
dramatically announce that I was leaving, and she would

shrug her shoulders. So I would leave. After a week or two I couldn't stand it any longer. I always went back.

When a fellow is in love, he does everything he can to attract his girl's attention, win her approval, make her laugh. My wife remembers that one day I went to call for her dressed all in green—green suit and hat, green shirt and tie, green socks. It was St. Patrick's Day, and I was trying to show her that I was as up-to-the-minute as any of the other sports she was going around with. She didn't understand the custom of wearing green; all she did was stand on the steps and laugh at me. "You look like a green pepper!" she said. Later, I remember, I was caught in the rain in that suit, and when it dried out it was two or three sizes too small.

Now, at that time I wore a mustache. I'd started to grow one in London, and kept it all through the army, and I still had it when I came to America. A waiter with a mustache could only work in places operated by Frenchmen and Italians. One day my Jenny and I had such a terrible quarrel I swore I would leave her forever. At the time there was a fellow I knew who'd been trying to persuade me to go with him to Pittsburgh. He said there were great opportunities out there, and that he had connections. As soon as I stomped out of the Bartholdi, I got in touch with him. "If you still want to go out West, let's go," I said. "I'm through with women and New York, too." There was only one hitch: he had no money. "Never mind," I said, "I'll pay your way." So we went to Pittsburgh. All during the train trip, I tried not to think of Jenny, but everything seemed to remind me of her. I thought of the walks we'd taken in Central Park, of the days we'd hired a boat and gone out on the lake up there, some of the shows we'd seen, the opera—all the good times. But mostly I thought of the way her eyes glowed when she smiled, and how pretty her little face was. By the time we reached Pittsburgh I was miserable. I was even more miserable when I got off the train and saw all that smoke and soot—for around that time, Pittsburgh deserved its old reputation. The smoke was like a fog. (Today, of course, it is much better.) The trip proved to be a complete disaster. None of the restaurants would hire a man with a mustache. My friend acted as a kind of valet for me, but that was about all he did do; most of the time he stayed in a hotel room, allowing me to pay his rent and buy his food. Pretty soon my money began to run out. On top of all that, I missed my girl so much it ached. One day, in desperation, I resolved I would get a job even if I had to shave off my mustache. So, I lathered up and scraped it off. Then I put it in an envelope and sent it to Jenny, to show her the bad condition I was in. I didn't enclose a letter—just the mustache. She told me later that when it came she was sure I would be home soon, and she was right. I came straight back to New York. She was sitting at the switchboard when I went upstairs at The Bartholdi. She'd never expected to see me that day. When I saw her face, I was so happy I could hardly talk—and I thought, from the way she looked, that she was glad to see me, too.

Now things began to go a little better with us. She did not exactly stop seeing other fellows, it's true, but she did give me more of her time. On Saturday nights we used to go to dances sponsored by Italian societies around New York—of course, we always got to them late, because both of us had to work. On Sundays we would take a few hours off in the afternoons and go up to Fort George Park or out to Coney Island on picnics. Mrs. Bartholdi was very nice to us—she encouraged us to go out together, and fostered the relationship. Sometimes she would have tickets to outings and parties, and when she did she often took us along with her. She was like a mother to us. She used to tell me I ought to invest in some of the Long Island real estate she was putting her money into, but I, with my cautious nature, always held off. Today I wish I had taken her advice. Some of the areas where she held lots later turned into well-populated residential districts.

All my life theater people have been influencing my decisions, and my courtship of Jenny was no exception. One

day she came to me, excited, and said, "Something wonderful
has happened!"

"What? What?"

"You know the Pathé people who stay at the Inn?"

Of course I knew them; I had taken care of them in the
restaurant many times. Pathé was one of the most active of
the movie companies. But something about her tone worried
me. "What is it? What about them?"

"They want me to be in the movies!" she cried. "They say
they will make another Pearl White out of me—why, what's
the matter?"

I must have been frowning. I didn't like the idea at all.
"Let's go for a walk," I said, "and talk about it."

She couldn't get away from her job just then, but she met
me in an hour, and we started to walk around. We were discussing the offer that had been made, and I was trying to
point out to her why it was a bad idea. I wasn't doing too
well—she was still excited. Her eyes were sparkling. Well, I
thought, this is the last straw. It's either going to be them or
me. I'm not going to have my wife on the screen, and that's
all there is to it. I didn't say any of this to her, because I
didn't want her to think I was trying to boss her around.
But I let her know that I meant it when I said I did not like
the idea.

All of a sudden it started to rain. We were at the corner
of Seventh Avenue and 53rd Street, and for shelter we ran
into a doorway. The rain came down in bucketfuls outside.
She came close to me, and I put my arm around her to shelter
her. That was when it happened. I proposed to her. I don't
remember what I said; all I know is that I said it as fast and
as persuasively as I could. To my great joy, she accepted.
And she also said she would not take the Pathé offer.

The first thing we did was tell Mrs. Bartholdi. She was
almost as delighted as we were. Pretty soon the word got
around among the guests, and then we took a terrible kidding—but we were both so happy, we didn't mind. In fact,

it was easier on me, because I wasn't working at the Bartholdi just then—I was working down at a place in the thirties.

"You'll have to be married in an actor's church," one of the guests said.

This suited both of us, so I went around to see the priest at St. Malachy's, where a good many stage and movie people were members. He said that we should be married in a church in our own district, and sent me to the Holy Cross Church, on 42nd Street, the one made famous by Father Duffy. There I sat down and explained to a priest that I wanted to get married. The priest's name sounded Italian to me, so I spoke to him in Italian. He listened to me for fifteen minutes and finally he said, "Well, I can't understand a word you're saying, but I gather that it has something to do with your wanting to get married."

"That's right," I said, switching to English.

"Where do you live?" he asked. I told him. "Sorry," he said, "but you'll have to be married in the Cathedral."

This second turn-down annoyed me. "Listen, Father," I said, "I am a Catholic. This is a Catholic church. I want to get married. If you won't marry me here, I'll have to go down to City Hall and get an official to do it. And if I do, you'll have to take the consequences. It won't be *my* fault."

"If that's your attitude," he said, "I suppose we can do it. But we'll have to post the banns—and that takes three weeks, you know."

"No," I said. "We want to do it next Monday."

"Maybe we could do that," he said.

Finally we got it settled. I couldn't help laughing a little, because I remembered the days at Dunwoody, and I thought, maybe it was a good thing that I didn't become a priest after all, since I've always had so many arguments with them.

Every happily married man remembers his bride as the prettiest woman he's ever seen, and I am no different. She wore a long white chiffon dress, and a straw hat with feathers, and I thought I was the luckiest fellow on earth. I had a black suit with a thin pencil stripe, and I had a straw hat, too. Just before the ceremony, while I was getting dressed, I had a small accident—I tore my pants at the knee as I was putting them on. But I sewed them up quickly and was all ready. Some friends of Jenny's, Mr. and Mrs. Frederick Costa, stood up for us during the ceremony. When the priest came to the part that goes "for better or for worse, in sickness and in health," Jenny said, "In sickness and in hell." The priest looked startled, and I nudged her. Later I twitted her about it, and she said, "You see, that meant I would stick to you no matter what you went through!"

After the ceremony I gave the priest $20 in an envelope. When Mr. Costa heard about that, he said it was too much. He even wanted to go and get part of it back. "No, no, let him have the twenty," I said. "I caused him enough trouble already."

Our honeymoon trip cost us twenty cents—ten cents on the subway, and ten cents on the trolley cars. We went to a country place called Sormani's, in the Bronx; we couldn't go any farther away from home because both of us had to be at work the very next day. But we made it quite a honeymoon, all the same. On the way to Sormani's we collected some friends, and by the time we arrived there our party had swelled to about twelve. They put down a wonderful luncheon, and everybody celebrated and drank wine and had a wonderful time. In the evening Jenny and I went out to watch the fireworks display at Palisades Park, across the Hudson, but we had to go back into the Inn when the mosquitoes became too inquisitive. The date was June 19, 1911.

The next day Jenny went back to her job at the Bartholdi, and I went back to mine at the place downtown, only to find that I'd been fired. I didn't care. I knew I would find another one in this great city of opportunity. I had my wife, my heart's desire. What did a job matter?

CHAPTER EIGHT

The First Sardi's

THE BIGGEST THRILL OF MY LIFE, after the thrill of my marriage to my dear Jenny, my admission to citizenship, and my becoming a father—this final thrill happened in 1921. Our very good friend Mario Cremona, who owned the small but charming restaurant called Mario's at 246 West 44th Street, had just built a new place, very original and artistic (he is artistically inclined) at 245 West 52nd Street, in a building which was later acquired by the Theatre Guild, on the spot where the ANTA Theatre stands today. Soon after he moved into his new place, Mario found that it required all his attention, and he decided to sell the old Mario's. He had many offers for it, but owing to our friendship of long standing—Mario too came from Canelli, and his family and mine had been close friends for a generation—he insisted that Jenny and I should have first chance at it. I will admit that at first it didn't strike me as a very good idea; I suppose it was the uncertainty of starting a new venture and the fact that I hated to leave the Palais Royale, which was a very good place to work. But Mario was insistent, and he also convinced Jenny—which was not so hard to do, because she had always had a flattering confidence in me, and was always telling me that I should start on my own. "I know you will make good," she would say. Still, I held back for a time. For one thing, I had been a partner in a small business before, and that venture had turned out so badly I do not even like to think about it today. For another, there were the children to consider: both of them were of school age, attending the Holy Cross Academy on 42nd Street, affiliated with the church where Jenny and I had been married. I certainly did not want to do anything to endanger their future. It was a big decision to make, but finally, after many talks with Jenny and my friend, I gave in. Mario's conditions for payments were very easy, and so I decided that I would try to justify the confidence he and my wife had in me, and put all the knowledge, experience, and hard work at my command into making a success of the venture. I soon found out that in spite of all this it was still an uphill struggle—but thanks to the encouraging words and down-to-earth good sense of my wife, I managed to hold on, trusting in God to help us and give us strength to continue.

Anybody is sentimental about his first possession of any kind—his first pair of long pants, his first watch, his first car. It's only natural. That is why I feel that the first Sardi's was one of the biggest thrills of my life. How proud Jenny and I were the day we took possession! When we walked in and looked around the room, we could hardly believe the place was ours. It was not very big; in fact, during the first few months I had a sign out front that said THE LITTLE RES-TAURANT. I thought this was appropriate because next door on the left was the Little Theater, run by Winthrop Ames. After a while we changed the sign to read SARDI'S, for that is what our regular customers always called the place. In the front was a tiny bar, which we used as a coffee counter and from which we served ice cream and salads—naturally, at the time, we could not use it as a bar, for Prohibition had already been made the law of the country. Behind it were the tables, and if I am not mistaken forty was the largest number we could take care of at one time. The walls were green, and I had hired an artist to paint romantic country scenes on them. We had a few potted palms scattered about here and there.

My wife and I found out at once that running our own place was not going to be easy. The work was hard and the hours were very long, and for the first couple of years we had no cook or chef. All the kitchen help we had was provided by a wonderfully intelligent and faithful Chinese boy named Chin. He was a great help to my wife, who had to cook and prepare almost everything, in addition to doing the marketing every morning. We had one waiter to start. His name was Carlo Oddone, and he too was a Piemontese. Today he is still with Sardi's, as a captain (he is the shortest man on our staff, and a great favorite with many customers). Carlo and I served the food in the dining room, but I had to double back to the kitchen to put the finishing touches on certain dishes before they were sent out to the customers.

In spite of all our work, we just could not seem to make ends meet. My payments to Mario were small and irregular, and although he was very patient and nice about it, I did not like to keep him waiting. One day, when I was going over our accounts, I knew I would have to make a decision.

"I am afraid we can't make a go of it," I said to Jenny. "Unless we get more business very soon, we will have to give up our place."

She wouldn't hear of it. "No, indeed," she said. "I know we can get ahead if we just manage to stick it out."

"Then," I said, "there is only one thing for me to do. I must get a job."

Luckily, I had heard that my good friend Arthur Coppel was in charge of the Rendezvous, a supper club in 45th Street. It was being operated by Gil Bogue and his wife, Gilda Gray. Bogue had been a partner at the Palais Royale, and I had known him well when I worked there. When I went to see him and told him I wanted to return to work, he seemed glad to see me and gave me a job right off. Well, that job turned out to be a lifesaver—that is, as long as I could stand it, because the schedule was quite severe.

As I said before, Jenny would do the marketing in the morning and then prepare all the sauces and the *plat du jour*. At mealtimes I went in the kitchen to serve the dishes that were ready and to cook the *à la carte* orders. (At the time our menu was not very large.) In the afternoons, after the luncheon trade had quieted down, I would leave things in the hands of Jenny and Chin and go upstairs to our apartment for a nap. In the evenings I would come down dressed in my tuxedo. I would take off the coat and put on a white jacket and serve dinner until a little before ten, when I would put the tuxedo coat back on and go across to 45th Street to take up my duties at the Rendezvous. There I would work most of the night. I never got home until around five A.M., and sometimes not until seven.

The job at the Rendezvous helped in two ways. First, I made very good money there; second, it gave me a chance to see a lot of people I had come to know at the Montmartre and the Palais Royale and to tell them that I was now in business for myself and would appreciate their patronage. First I asked Gil Bogue if it would be all right to let the people know—and to my surprise, he not only said it would be all right, but he told more people about my little place than I did myself! So did Arthur Coppel and a colleague of mine named Zani. (You see, our place was not in competition with the Rendezvous, for they served only supper there.) Gil Bogue and Gilda Gray came to dine with us often, and brought many of their friends. They used to like to sit in the garden we had made in the back yard. The garden was Jenny's idea. Carlo and I built supports for an awning, some tables and benches, and some cages for pigeons and rabbits. A waiter friend of mine named Conti, who had retired and moved to a farm in New Jersey, had given our children two rabbits for Easter, and they began to multiply almost as soon as we got them. Then, too, we had some pullets in the cages.

What with the rabbits, the chickens and pigeons and the dog that Carlo gave Cino, it was like a farmyard in the garden. One of the rabbits grew to be the biggest I ever saw, and certainly the boldest. Sometimes customers would open the door to his cage, and he would jump down and hop around from table to table, not afraid of anybody. If a cat came near him, he stood his ground; if you went after him with a broom, he would bite at the straw. People used to order lettuce especially for him. He was so daring, we named him Ardito. We also had a good many stray alley cats that came to see what was going on in the garden; no matter how hard we tried, we never were able to get rid of them. One evening, when Gil Bogue and Gilda Gray were having their dinner in the garden, a cat fight arose in the next yard. How those cats went at each other! It sounded like there were twenty or thirty of them, and the next thing Gil Bogue knew, a half dozen of them came swarming over the fence and fell right on his table, clawing and spitting at each other! Of course, he took it as a big joke, and he always laughed when he told about it.

Now, along with the customers Gil Bogue sent us, other people I had known began showing up. Paul Whiteman, whom I have mentioned before, began coming in with his musicians, Mike Pingatore, Henry Busse, the one they called Pee Wee and all the rest, whose names I no longer remember. I had met Paul at the Palais Royale. Another friend of that period began coming in, too—Alex Hanlon, a theatrical agent who did much of the booking for Loew's State. Frank D'Amore, the acrobat I'd met at the Palais Royale, also began coming to see us. All of these people brought friends, and the friends brought other friends, and before too long our business began to get a little better.

But while the cash register was getting healthier, I was not. Those hours at the Rendezvous were beginning to take a heavy toll. I believe I worked there for about nine weeks before my physical condition began to suffer, and then it was clear that I could not go on. With reluctance, I had to tell Gil Bogue that I was leaving him. Those nine weeks at the Rendezvous helped me more than I can say; in addition to meeting my obligations, I was able to afford to hire our first chef. Now, with our Chinese boy, we had two men working in the kitchen, and so as business continued good I decided to hire another waiter for the dining room. The man I chose from the applicants was Lorenzo Robotti, and I suppose I do not have to say that he was a Piemontese, too, like the rest of us. Some time after Lorenzo came we also hired his brother, Giovanni, who is still with us as I write these lines. Lorenzo would be with us today, too, I am sure, but he died a few years ago. To Jenny and me it was a profound loss, for in the time he was with us he became our very good friend. After Giovanni began in the dining room we hired another waiter, and then a salad man for the kitchen. By the time the old Sardi's was operating at its peak, in its very best days, we had six people in the kitchen and twelve waiters —and that was about as large a staff as our place could hold.

If there was one person alone who was responsible for theatrical people flocking to our place in great numbers, credit would have to be given a man who was not a theatrical personage at all—although he did love the theater and liked the company of actors and actresses. He was a fine Southern gentleman, Naval Commander V. V. Woodward, who once had been chief engineer aboard the *Leviathan*. Commander Woodward was an active member of The Lambs, the theatrical men's club located east of our place in the next block of 44th Street. He came in for dinner one evening, enjoyed himself, and returned every night for a week. Then he began telling his friends at The Lambs about us, and they began coming in to dine in groups. The next thing we knew, our place had a nickname: Commander Woodward and his friends were referring to it as "The Lambs' Annex." We could never repay him for what he did for us, for at that time business really did pick up. Along with the commander, there were several other young naval officers who began coming in. Some of them lived up the street near the corner of Broadway, in an apartment building called Westover Court. One of these naval officers, R. Nelson Hickman, an old customer of mine, last year wrote me a letter reminiscing about that apartment house and the old Sardi's. Westover Court was a gold mine of talent, and among its tenants were several who later became famous. S. N. Behrman and Philip Barry, then struggling playwrights, lived there; so did Roland Young, who was just making his mark in *The Better 'Ole,* and the now-famous Philip Merivale. All of them came down the street to eat with us, and Hickman, my correspondent, remembers that Philip Barry sometimes brought along his manuscripts and read them over while he was having his dinner.

Our 44th Street clientele was not limited to the struggling actors, however, not by a long shot! We came to the attention of some of the most important producing people, too. The first really great name in the theater to discover us was Winthrop Ames, who at that time was operating the Little Theatre, a few doors away. Mr. Ames, a handsome man with a patrician face, came from an old aristocratic New England family, but despite his background he was as friendly a fellow as I've ever known. He had been interested in the theater from his earliest youth; as a student at Harvard, he had written a show, *Proserpina,* for production by the Hasty Pudding Club. Because his family was opposed to his making a career of the theater, he became an editor of architectural and art magazines in Boston. Finally he could not stand it any longer; the pull of the stage was too strong for him. With a man named Loren F. Deland, he established in 1905 a stock company that played in the Castle Square Theatre in Boston. In 1908 Lee Shubert went to Boston to induce him to come to New York as general manager of a project to be called the New Theatre, which was set up in a new building at 60th Street and Central Park West (it later became known as the Century Theatre). John Corbin was to be literary manager of the enterprise. The situation appealed to Mr. Ames, and his New York career began. The New Theatre was the first effort to establish an American repertory company. Among the plays produced there were *The Winter's Tale,* done for the first time in this country in the Shakespearean manner; Maurice Maeterlinck's *Sister Beatrice* and *The Blue Bird,* John Galsworthy's *Strife,* Sir Arthur Wing Pinero's *The Thunderbolt,* and Sheridan's *The School for Scandal,* along with many, many others. When our restaurant opened, Mr. Ames' reputation was already secure in theatrical history. By that time he had left the New Theatre to build and manage the Little Theatre, and the Booth Theatre in the same block on 45th Street, just across Shubert Alley. He formulated many plans for productions in our place and brought in with him many of the most famous actors of all time, including George Arliss, who appeared for him in William Archer's *The Green Goddess,* and in Galsworthy's *Old English,* two of Arliss' biggest successes. Later, Arliss appeared for him in *The Merchant of Venice.* I remember that we took our children to see Mr. Ames' production of *Snow White,* which if I am not mistaken was the first play in New York produced especially for children. During World War I, Mr. Ames was associated briefly with E. H. Sothern, the veteran English actor, whose first American successes had been made with Charles Frohman's Lyceum Company, and who for years headed a Shakespearean repertory company with his wife, Julia Marlowe. Together, they sponsored two theaters in France for American soldiers. Mr. Ames' productions are too numerous to set down here, but I remember particularly *Beggar on Horseback,* by George S. Kaufman and Marc Connelly, Clemence Dane's *Will Shakespeare,* and Alice Brown's *Children of the Earth.*

In addition to actors who were working for him, Mr. Ames also brought with him many of his associates, among them Johnson Briscoe, his casting director. At the time I had a little *grappa* in the place, and whenever there was a celebration or some special occasion, I would send a pony to my friends' table. *Grappa* is connected with my earliest childhood; I remember how my grandfather always made his own, and how they always had a big party each year when the new *grappa* was ready for consumption. Once, in the army, I brought a big bottle back to my company. Those officers drank it with such religion! "Ah," they said, "it is better than fine champagne!" Well, Mr. Ames, Johnson Briscoe, and all the rest felt the same way about it. Briscoe gave it a nickname. Because it was so strong, he called it "Fourth of July."

Another associate of Mr. Ames' first came in soon after we opened. His name was Guthrie McClintic, and he and his wife, Katharine Cornell, are among the best friends my wife and I ever made in the theater. Mr. McClintic recalls seeing me first at the Palais Royale, but I must confess I do not remember him from there. Rather, I recall that he came to see us first with Henry Hull, the actor; they came in late one night, and one of them had a flask. I sometimes allowed my favorite customers to bring their own whisky into the place; since I didn't sell it, it was the least I could do. However, I was always a little nervous about it, and I asked them to please use coffee cups for the liquor; they did not object, for which I was very grateful. That first night Mr. McClintic and Hull stayed very late. From then on, Mr. McClintic came in frequently with Bert Savoy, a well-known comic of the day. Savoy was a funny man offstage as well as on, and he used to keep us all laughing with his jokes and capers. He used to say that if the Statue of Liberty knew how wicked New York really was, she would dive right into New York harbor. He was very well known as a female impersonator, and was a leading member of *The Greenwich Village Follies*. Unfortunately he died suddenly before he had a chance to achieve the success he might have made. In 1923 he and a friend, Jack Grossman, known on the stage as Jack Vincent, were walking along the beach at Long Beach, Long Island, watching a furious thunderstorm that had arisen like a cyclone. As they were strolling along, watching the storm, a bolt of lightning struck them both, killing them instantly. Neither body was marked in any way. There was great sadness in show business when Savoy was killed. Eddie Cantor sent a wire to his relatives that said, "The whole world will miss his laughter."

But to return to Mr. McClintic. He was a protégé of Winthrop Ames (and, by the way, said recently that he is going to write a book about the producer, who died in 1937). He had first come to the stage in 1914, appearing as a messenger in a play called *The Truth*. After appearing in several other plays, he went with Mr. Ames in 1918 as a stage manager. After a few years he became a producing manager on his own. In 1925 he had three productions going at once: *Mrs. Partridge Presents, All Dressed Up,* and Michael Arlen's *The Green Hat,* one of Miss Cornell's most famous roles of all time. They were married in 1921, and from the beginning they were in our place regularly. While *The Green Hat* was running, Miss Cornell's popularity was tremendous (of course, it is still tremendous!). After each performance she was nearly mobbed at the stage door. Her husband used to rush her down the street to our place, where the crowds would not disturb her. She and my wife would sit for hours talking by the fireplace. The McClintics have moved to the country now, but whenever they are in the city and have some special occasion to observe, they still visit Sardi's. I remember that one of the first times Mrs. Eleanor Roosevelt was in the place, she came with Mr. McClintic; it was the year Mildred Natwick won the award of the Barter Theatre for her performance in *Saturday's Children.* Mrs. Roosevelt, McClintic, Clifton Webb, and Robert Porterfield, head of the Barter Theatre, held a celebration with us.

It was people like the McClintics, Mr. Ames, and others who followed them in who gave the old place its family atmosphere. Lee Shubert began coming to see us regularly, and when he could not get away from his business we would send him dinner to his apartment atop his Shubert Theatre. Another one of the early-day regulars was John Golden, the producer. I have more to say about John Golden later on in the book, but now, while I am remembering the old place, I do recall that he was one of my wife's greatest admirers. He said she had had the most beautiful hair he had ever seen— and of course, I agreed with him; Jenny's hair looks like spun silver-white silk. One day I put him at a table near the front. He would not sit there. "How can I look at your wife's hair from far up there?" he demanded.

John Drew took to coming to see us regularly; of course we had known him back in the Bartholdi Inn days. We felt honored, for there were few actors of the time who were more distinguished. He had appeared for Charles Frohman, in several plays with Maude Adams, both here and abroad. But although he was a lordly figure, an actor of the old school, son of a famous stage family, he was no more snobbish than the stagehands who ate with us. He used to love to talk to my wife and me in Italian. When our summer garden was open, customers had to reach it by going through the kitchen. Quite often my wife or I would be working in there. John Drew would always stop and chat with us. A couple of times, as I remember, he would begin on his antipasto while he was standing there talking.

There was always a good deal of horseplay in the old place, for the theater was booming and spirits were high. I had installed a lawn sprinkler over the awning that covered the garden, connecting it to the bathroom in our apartment on the third floor of the building. Sometimes, while people were eating there, I would run upstairs and turn on the water. Hearing the noise, the customers would think it was raining outside. What a surprise they would get when they went out into the street and found it clear! One day A. E. Anson, the English actor who scored a hit with Laurette Tay-

lor in *The Furies*, was sitting in the garden when we turned
the sprinkler on. He and his companion, Marjorie Rambeau,
remarked on the rain and went on with their conversation.
A moment after they left, Anson stepped back into the dining room and said to Carlo, "Blasted funny, old man—it's
raining in the rear but not in the front!"

The horseplay aside, there was a good deal of serious business conducted around Sardi's tables. Actors' Equity had
been organized two years before we opened, during the celebrated Actors' Strike of 1919, and many of the officials of
that organization would come into our place and discuss
matters pertaining to the welfare of their members. Francis
E. Wilson, the star of *Lightnin'*, was in often, along with
Frank Gilmore, Bert Lytell, and many other prominent
Equity people. For a long time the only advertisement I ever
placed in any publication with any degree of regularity was
the one I put in the Equity newspaper, and every day we
would send a Sardi menu to be posted on the Equity bulle-
tin board.

The theater was at its best in those days of the twenties.
There were over sixty legitimate houses in the Broadway
section at that time, and it was not uncommon for two hundred fifty-odd productions to come to town during a single
season. It saddens me to think how the living stage has de-
clined; in the 1951-52 season, there were only twenty-one
theaters remaining, and only seventy-four productions came
in. Many of the fine old houses have been given over to television or to the movies. Yet it doesn't pay to cry, and even
as this book is going to press, there are signs that the theater
is coming back. There is a movement afoot to change the
New York building code so that more theaters may be erected,
and a few houses which were taken over by the movie chains
have been reconverted. Yet even if the theater returns to its
former glory, I doubt if there will ever be a period as exciting as the early years of Sardi's existence. What plays there
were, and such actors! In one night in our place it was not

unusual to see Walter Houston, Marie Dressler, Josephine Hull, Osgood Perkins (one of our best friends; we were very sad at the time of his death), all three Barrymores, John Devereux, Leslie Howard, and Maurice Evans. Richard Bennett often came in, and so did Charles Coburn, Victor McLaglen, Dudley Digges, Robert Loraine, William Keefe, Brandon Peters, Martin Flavin, Florence Reed, Jane Cowl, Lila Lee, Lillian Gish, Vivienne Segal, Eddie Dowling, Sydney Greenstreet, Lionel Atwill, Charles Winninger, and—well, this is beginning to sound like a gossip column! The writers came to see us, too; I remember particularly Ring Lardner, who usually sat by himself and seldom spoke to anyone except his waiter and me; George Jean Nathan and H. L. Mencken, the famous editors of the old *Smart Set* magazine; a young red-haired fellow, just beginning to establish himself as one of America's foremost novelists, Sinclair Lewis; and playwrights such as Frederick Arnold Kummer, Bayard Viellier, and Rachel Crothers. Because the big names came to us, the lesser-known people began coming, too. Many of our friends began leaving messages to each other, and some would use our place as a mail address—occasionally we had as many as forty or fifty letters waiting to be picked up. It got so that many actors and actresses would sometimes call up from out of town, on tour, just to find out what was going on and to hear the latest gossip; there was always someone around willing to fill them in. Sometimes the calls from out of town were cries for help—actors would be stranded by a show that closed, and would call for money to come home. I remember many collections that were taken up and sent out to unfortunates; one of our regulars would go from table to table, passing the hat, and soon the necessary amount would be subscribed.

The atmosphere in the old place was so pleasant, and so like that of a home, that Jenny and I often allowed the children to come down and meet some of the friends. No two children, I suppose, were ever privileged to know so many famous people of the theater. Many customers would make a beeline for the boy and girl the minute they arrived. Florence Reed used to say that Anna looked exactly as she had when she was a little girl, and Mark Hellinger, then a columnist and later a movie producer, often said he wished the children were his (that was long before he married Gladys Glad, the famous Follies beauty; and by the way, they celebrated their wedding in the new Sardi's—it was one of the first big parties we had in the place). Whenever our dear friend Helen Keller came in, she always asked that the children be brought to her table. She would touch their faces, and you could see that she was fixing their features in her mind. "Such beautiful children," she would say. Winthrop Ames was very fond of the children, too, and it was he and Frank Craven and Wally Ford who encouraged us to allow little Cino to appear in several productions. When it came time for the boy to make his first appearance, he was so familiar with the stage and the theatrical life that he was no more nervous than he would have been in a marble game out on the sidewalk. He walked on, said his lines like a real trouper, and made Jenny and me very proud of him. His notices were good, too.

As time went on, Sardi's became a kind of property room for theaters in the neighborhood. In 1922, when *Seventh Heaven* opened at the Booth, we supplied fake wine, cognac, salami, and French bread for every performance, and from then on other producers and directors began requesting the same service. When actors heard that we would send food out, we begain doing a brisk business delivering dinners to dressing rooms on matinee days, when the stars did not want to leave the theaters between shows. If I am not mistaken, Edmund Gwenn was one of the first of our customers for whom we did this small favor. The late Gertrude Lawrence always insisted on having a Sardi dinner sent to her. Today, Cino has carried on the custom for younger stars, such as Vanessa Brown and Geraldine Brooks and other members of the "family." Then, too, there was another service we supplied, although it was not exactly a function of the restaurant. We had a pair of cab drivers who always stood outside the place. Although we never knew their last names, we called them Big Irving and Little Irving. They knew all our customers, and often would drive them straight to their doors without being told where to go. When we moved up the street to the new place, Big Irving and Little Irving moved right along.

As the twenties went on, our business got better and better. Then in 1925 I had a cablegram from one of my sisters saying that Mother was very ill. My wife and I had been planning to go back to Italy for a visit, but we quickly decided that I should go right away and that she would follow with the children. Within twenty-four hours I got my passport and booked passage on the *Paris*. My family at that time was still living in Genoa. I got to the city around ten at night and went immediately to my mother's house. My sister took me into her room. My mother was so still, lying there in bed, so frail and wasted, that I was sure her condition was critical. She opened her eyes, looked up at me, and said only, "My, isn't he a fine-looking man." Her voice was so low we could scarcely make out the words. I tried to get her to talk, but she was too far gone.

Domenico, my brother who was the actor, had flown home the day before from Tripoli, where he had been appearing in a play. We decided that the doctor who had been treating Mother had not been doing enough, so we called in three of Genoa's leading physicians. They gave us no hope. They told the family doctor that he should not have allowed her to become so run down. "She is too weak to save," one said. The following night she lost consciousness, and a few hours later she died. We never did find out exactly what had caused her sickness.

Naturally I wanted to take the body home to Canelli. The next day some Franciscan monks in the church next door to my mother's house held a service for her, and at five A.M. the morning after that we started the journey. At home in Canelli there was another funeral service which Uncle Pietro had arranged.

After we had seen my mother to the cemetery, Domenico asked me what I was going to do. The question came as a surprise. It had not occurred to me to do anything but return to America. Although I had always thought in the back of my mind that I might some day come home to Italy, since Jenny and I had been married, I had not given it much serious thought. Following the hearse to Canelli in the funeral procession, passing over the familiar land of my boyhood, I had left no urge to return. And now that I was home, the customs seemed strange to me. I could not understand how that doctor could have allowed my mother to grow weak; nothing of that kind happened in America. It was hard for me, as it had been when I came home from London, to get used to the fashion of speaking with the hands. And, of all things, I missed the drinking water! There was an abundance of good Canelli wine, but I had fallen out of the habit of drinking wine all the time. One afternoon in Genoa I got so thirsty for water I rushed down to the railroad station, bought a quart bottle, and drank it all down.

Thinking over these things, and feeling the strangeness, I realized that Italy was no longer my home. I had become an American, through and through. When Jenny, Cino, and Anna arrived, I was ready to pack them up and go right back to the United States. We visited her family at Castel Alfero, near Torino, and we traveled around a little on a vacation, but I was restless. Only when I got to Milano, which was full of movement and reminded me of New York, was I happy. I could not wait to go home. Big things were going to happen to me, I thought. When we left Italy, I thought to myself, "Good-by forever."

CHAPTER NINE

The New Sardi's

THINGS BEGAN GOING VERY WELL for my wife and me when we returned from our trip to Europe. We had two fine children, nice quarters in the apartment above the restaurant, and the grandest collection of friends any couple could ever want. On top of that, our business was very good. We were very, very happy—so happy, in fact, that at night, when I said my prayers, I always remembered to thank the Lord for His kindness, as though I was afraid He might take His blessings away.

Then, in 1926, it looked for a while as though our happy existence might come to end. Our landlord, Vincent Astor, had given an option on our building to A. H. Erlanger, who was planning to build a new theater on the site. Erlanger had bought up several other adjacent buildings, and he was ready to tear them all down. We would have to move.

That was the time when we found out how kind our friends were. Several of them, including Winthrop Ames, declared that they would try to buy the building from Astor so that we could stay in our location. Unfortunately there was nothing to be done. Erlanger held the option, and he was planning to exercise his rights. The theater he built, by

the way, is now known as the St. James. Our restaurant was
located right about where the stage is today.

As soon as I heard the news, I got busy looking for a new
building. I didn't want to move out of the neighborhood, if
I could help it, and in fact I didn't want to move out of 44th
Street. But although we made inquiries up and down the
block, there was nothing to be found. The next best thing,
I thought, would be to move into the corresponding block
on 45th Street, for after all the famous Shubert Alley ran
between and almost made one big street out of 44th and 45th.
Our faithful customers would not mind walking another
block, I reasoned. Soon after I had come to this conclusion,
I ran into a man I knew who owned four buildings on 45th.
After listening to my predicament, he offered to rent me one
of them.

"One won't be enough," I said. "I'll need two houses, at
least."

"That can be arranged," he said.

I had a look at the houses, and they seemed suitable. Right
away, then, I took my future son-in-law, Frank Gina, over to
make an inspection, and I commissioned him to draw up
plans for a new, bigger, and better Sardi's. Frank, a member
of the architectural firm of Ketchum, Gina, and Sharp, went
right to work, and within a week he had plans, blueprints,
and everything ready. I planned to spend around $25,000 or
$30,000 in remodeling. My wife and I thought we would
make everything new—even the tablecloths, the silver, and
the china. We were so enthusiastic that I wanted to begin
letting contracts for the work as soon as Frank brought us
the plans. Before I could do that, however, I had to sign the
lease which my landlord-to-be had promised me.

My lawyer, Joe Adelson, made an appointment with the
landlord's lawyer, and together we went to his office for the
formal signing. I do not recall the date, but I do remember
that it was the last day of a six-day bicycle race. The landlord's lawyer was a great bicycle-racing fan, and as soon as

we arrived at his office he told us he wanted to get the business over with as rapidly as possible, so he could get off to
see the finish. As it turned out, the landlord was late. While
we were waiting for him, his lawyer was getting more and
more impatient. Finally he looked at me and said, "Are you
sure you want this fellow as a landlord? You're certainly getting the worst landlord in New York!"

Neither Adelson nor I knew what to make of this; we
were so puzzled we didn't know what to say. While we were
staring at each other, wondering what had prompted the
lawyer to say such a thing, the landlord arrived.

He came in very quickly, apologized for being late, and
asked his lawyer if the papers were ready.

"You mean the lease, I suppose," I said. "I hope you have
made it for a long term, because I am going to spend quite
a bit of money on the alterations and furnishings."

To my surprise, the man said, "You aren't getting a lease,
Sardi—only an agreement. What if I would sell the property?
In that case you would have to move on thirty days' notice."

I looked at Adelson, and he looked at me, and he said,
"No wonder we were warned about this man."

"You promised me a lease," I said to the landlord.

"No, no, I never promised," he said.

We asked one last question—if he really meant that he
would not grant me a lease (you see, we were so stunned we
still thought he might be joking).

"Absolutely not," he said. "I will not give you a lease, and
that's final."

There was nothing for us to do but take our hats and go,
but not before I told the man what I thought of him.

I was so disappointed that when I got home it was some
time before I could tell Jenny the sad news. When I did,
she came through for me as she always did. She refused to be
discouraged. "Something will happen," she said. "Wait and
see—it will work out." But as the days passed, and we sat
down each evening after the dinner hour to discuss our prob-

lem, there seemed to be no solution. The day on which we were scheduled to move was coming closer and closer, and I was afraid that I would have to go back to working as a captain in someone else's place.

It was on one of those evenings, while we were sitting at our usual table, feeling gloomy and hopeless, that a wonderful thing happened. A gentleman came in and said he wanted to talk to me. I asked him to sit down at our table, and Jenny got up to leave.

"Please stay, Mrs. Sardi," the gentleman said. "I'm sure you will be interested in what I have to say."

The gentleman introduced himself as Herbert Krapp and said that he was the architect for Lee Shubert. His first words filled us with hope.

"I am here to tell you," he said, "that you might not have to move from 44th Street after all. Mr. Lee has watched you and your wife—how you work, the way you conduct your restaurant, and he wants to help you. He wants you to stay on 44th Street."

It all seemed like a dream to me. As soon as I recovered from my astonishment, I asked how it would be possible. Mr. Krapp then explained that a few doors east of us, between the Winthrop Ames Little Theatre and the Shuberts' 44th Street Theatre, the Shuberts had owned a building which they had torn down in order to build a small theater. Now they had changed their minds and were not going to erect the theater after all. Instead, they would make this space available to me for a restaurant!

"Tell me what you would like," Mr. Krapp continued, "and the plans will be drawn up and building will be started at once, so that you can move into your new place in around three months' time."

Jenny and I felt so happy that we wanted to dance. The very next day I sent my lawyer to see Mr. Kline, the Shuberts' attorney. He told my lawyer that Mr. Lee had told him to give us a nice long lease and to tell me not to worry

about ever having to move from 44th Street, for as long as
he lived I would have a friend. When I heard that, I was
glad that we had done our best to make our place a good
one. Lee Shubert had dined with us often, sometimes by
himself and sometimes with some of his friends, such as John
Golden, Mr. Ames, or Arthur Hopkins, and I was pleased
that we had made such a good impression.

As soon as the lease was signed Jenny and I began making
our plans all over again. We decided that we would like to
have a main dining room on the first floor, a private banquet
room on the second floor with sliding doors that would par-
tition the room off for parties, and a roof garden with elevator service. To my delight, word came back that all this
would be built as we wished. But then there were a few disappointments. First, construction was started later than
originally planned. Then, when the steel structure got up
to the third floor, somebody decided that the building would
be made into a five-story structure. When the framework
got up to five, plans were changed again. Now it would be
seven. Even that was not the end. Before the workers were
finished, they had put up an eleven-story office building. That
meant that I did not get the roof garden I had hoped for;
there was an apartment for J. J. Shubert on the top floor.

Thus it was more than a year before my wife and I were
able to take possession of the new Sardi's. I was worried during that year, for I was afraid that I would lose contact with
my customers and that they would forget me. I wrote to
them all, telling them that I would be back in business soon.
But meanwhile, something else happened that almost proved
disastrous. It is impossible for a man in his thirties to be idle
for a year, particularly if he has worked hard since boyhood,
and for this reason I was anxious to get working again. While
I'd been in Italy, some friends had written me that they
knew of a good location for a restaurant downtown on Park
Place, and they urged me to go into the venture with them.
I did, and although we ran the place for a time, we could

not make a go of it. For one thing, it was too large. For another, the place had seen better days. For another, I felt out of place downtown; and I didn't know the clientele, and I missed 44th Street and my theatrical friends. On top of all that, first one and then the other partner pulled out of the arrangement. I was stubborn, and I wanted to carry out my obligations, so I stayed on until I almost went broke. Today Jenny hates even the mention of that place downtown, and I must say I don't blame her. It nearly ruined us.

My only contact with the theatrical world during those dismal days came about through a restaurant that might have been called "The Substitute Sardi's." After we closed the old place, some of the waiters—Giovanni and Lorenzo Robotti, and another named Louis—had rented a little place on 45th Street. My wife and I gave them all the dishes, glassware, and silver from our establishment, and they managed to attract some of our customers. I used to go over and sit in their place in the evenings; it cheered me a little to talk to them and to the stage people who came in. The boys felt that running a restaurant was not to their taste, however, and when we finally opened the new Sardi's, they came back to work for us. Right here I should say a word or two about the faithfulness of our waiters. Philip Theophilades, Frank Rossetto, and John Bosco came to work for us shortly after we opened the new place and are still going strong today. John Delsy and John Poggi have been with us more than fifteen years; in fact, some of us think of Felix Appino, Angelo Olivio, Duilio Botta, Peter Trocea, and Vincent Caniggia as comparative newcomers, because they've only been with us ten years or more! Fathers and sons have worked in our place. Many men who started out as bus boys or kitchen helpers are now in jobs of real authority; Jimmy Malinsky, who is *maître d'* in the main dining room for luncheon and dinner, began as a bartender's assistant and worked his way up; and Angelo Berna, who began with us twelve years ago as a bus boy, is now our steward. George Pappas, whom everybody calls Georgie, has worked for us as a bus boy for more than twenty years. I call him "The Professional Insulter," because he always pretends to be indignant about something or other. After Georgie had been with us for quite a few years, I suggested to him that he ought to train to become a waiter. "That's an insult!" he cried. "I wouldn't associate with those shoemakers!"

All our old waiters, and the new ones, too, are part of the Sardi family; they have learned, time and again, that because they take care of the customers as they would their own relatives, the customers always take care of them. One night a drunk wandered into the place and demanded a table from Felix Appino, the supper-hour *maître d'*. Felix, the personification of politeness, would never have refused to serve the man, but he wanted to make sure that there would be no trouble. As a waiter was escorting the drunk to an out-of-the-way table, Felix signaled to the bartender, indicating that no drinks should be served. The man happened to look up just then and saw Felix signaling in the mirror. He turned upon Felix and began getting nasty. Suddenly he was confronted by a huge, dangerous-looking man. It was Lionel Stander, then appearing across the street at the Broadhurst in the revival of John O'Hara's *Pal Joey*. Stander, who did not come onstage in the show until the second act, would wait every evening in Sardi's until it was time for him to go to work. He bundled the offensive man out into the street before the latter knew what was happening.

But to get back to my story. After what seemed like ages, we were finally able to move into our new building—but even then, the rest of it wasn't finished! The date was March 5, 1927, and that is when the history of the present Sardi's officially began. But there was one more disappointment. I had contracted for some big refrigerators, some air-conditioning machines, and some ice-making machines, but when they were delivered we discovered that, of all things, there was no basement to the building! Naturally, this cost us considerable valuable space in the kitchen, for that was the only place we had to put the machines—and some of the equipment had to be modified in order to fit in. Later, when business got better, this proved to be a big handicap; and it was not solved until after I turned the restaurant over to Cino. He attacked the problem by renting some space on the third floor.

Jenny and I were very proud of the new Sardi's. I had furnished it in the London manner, so that it partially resembled some of the places I'd worked in over there—paneled walls, warm carpet on the floor, good sturdy mahogany chairs, and the very finest tablecloths, glassware, silver, and china. In my original plans, I had wanted a circular staircase leading up to the second floor. The idea had been approved by the contractors at first, but then they had decided against it; for a long time, our second floor could only be reached by elevator in the lobby just west of our main entrance. Since we did not get our staircase, our plans were left with a space too big to be a lobby and too small to be much of anything else. I didn't want a lobby that big, so I compromised by putting the checkroom in there. That was where Renee Carroll, who became famous all over the country, acquired her reputation as the foremost hat-check girl in the United States.

For some time before I opened the new Sardi's, many of my friends had been urging me to sell whisky there. I still refused; I told them all the same thing—I would not break the law. Then, one day some time after we opened, I had some pressure from another source. Two hoodlums came in one day and said, "We want to have a look at your beer pipes to see if they need repair." I had no beer pipes; I knew the men were members of a mob, looking for a shakedown for "protection." I admit that I was frightened. Then help came to me from an unexpected source. Texas Guinan, the fabulous night-club and speak-easy hostess, was a customer and a friend of ours. Everybody thought of Texas as a wild, hell-raising flapper; her cry of "Hello, Sucker!" was something of a symbol of the twenties. But my wife and I knew her as a very decent girl who did not drink, who lived quietly with her parents in Greenwich Village, and who was very nice, almost motherly, to the girls who worked in the chorus lines in her clubs (many of those girls later became famous; among them are Ruby Keeler, Claire Luce, Barbara Stanwyck, Olive Thomas, Irene Delroy, and Eleanor Brooks). When Texas was playing in *The Padlocks of 1927*, at the Shubert, across the street from our place, they used to carry her out into the street on their shoulders at intermission. She would point at our place and shout, "Now go and eat at Sardi's, Suckers!" Well, word got to Texas that the hoodlums had visited me. I am told that she then told her brother Tommy about the visit. He had many acquaintances in the underworld. Some time later the hoodlums came back to see me; not only the first two, but many others, besides. They never mentioned the beer pipes again. They behaved like perfect gentlemen, sitting quietly, talking to their girls and to each other, never causing a bit of trouble. In many ways they were the best-behaved customers we had—and all because Texas Guinan had told them to be good!

I held to my resolve not to sell liquor all through Prohibition. After Repeal, I reluctantly put in a bar—but I made a resolution that it was going to be the smallest one possible. Therefore, I moved Renee's checkroom out of that little space just next to the lobby and put the bar in there. We called it the Little Bar, with a sign announcing it as such outside. Soon it became a curiosity—I suppose it was one of the smallest bars in New York—and around the time of the cocktail hour, it was always jammed. It looked as though only ten or twelve people could get into it, but as many as thirty or forty used to crowd their way inside.

Because the Little Bar was so small, and because of its shape, the people who patronized it made up a kind of in-formal club. The semicircular shape made it possible for them to talk across to each other. Thus an outsider, elbowing his way to the slab, would find himself caught in a cross-current of conversation. This would give him the idea that he had intruded upon some sort of private gathering, and he would not stay long. This suited the regular club members very well. They thought of themselves as a kind of aristocracy of Sardi's, and it was not often that one of their number condescended to sit down in the restaurant proper.

According to Bert McCord, the theatrical correspondent of the New York *Herald Tribune,* who once devoted his entire column to the Little Bar, the principal club members were Tom Ewell, who last season scored the biggest hit of his career in George Axelrod's play, *The Seven-year Itch;* Eddie Diamond, a stage manager; Bernard Hart, known as Bernie, an incurable punster and a successful producer (brother of Moss Hart, the playwright); Philip Coolidge and Jack Sheehan and David Orrick and David Wayne, actors; Fred Spooner, a press agent; and Saki Oura, a sound technician. Even though the Little Bar is no more—the checkroom has again replaced it—these same boys still come around nearly every day. The main club members are often joined by three other regulars, when they are not in Hollywood—Rex Harrison, John Carradine, and Melville Cooper. Oddly enough, two charter members of the fraternity—Tommy Ewell and Fred Spooner—never drink anything stronger than soft drinks. When the Little Bar was flourishing, it served as a message center for the regulars.

As I have said, it is a rare day when one of the Little Bar boys sit down at a table. When they sit down at all, they use the stairs which now lead to the second floor (we no longer have to send our customers into the lobby to take the elevator, thank goodness). They have always remained a little aloof from the other customers, and even from me—as a matter of fact, what little I know about them, I've learned from Bert McCord! The walls of the stairway on which the members of the club sit are decorated with a collection of photographs of many of our friends. Some of them were willed me by

Harriet Underhill, the critic, another regular customer. One of my favorite pictures in this Sardi gallery is that of José Ferrer made up for *Cyrano*. At one side of the frame is a little square extension, to accommodate the enormous nose he wore in that production. One night Jimmy Durante came in with some friends. The first thing he saw was the nose in its special frame. He touched his own nose and cried in mock indignation, "The man's an imposter!"

For a time, the top of the stairs was guarded by Pero, a parrot which one of my sisters gave the children. Pero was not very talented, considering that he was a theatrical restaurant's pet; he could voice the usual request for a cracker, but that was about all except for a maniacal laugh which, as my daughter Anna said, sounded like something out of *The Bat*. Pero was not too friendly with our customers, but he was on the best of terms with a cat we had. The cat liked to climb up on his cage, reach in, and bat him playfully with his paws, and Pero in turn would snap at his playmate's tail. One day, when a waiter opened the door to the cage, Pero climbed out and perched on top. The cat took one look at him and jumped inside the cage. They resumed their game with their usual positions reversed, and from then on it was a regular routine they went through every day. Soon after we got Pero, my wife bought some canaries and placed their cages around the second-floor dining room. "If you are going to have birds, you will have to take care of them," I told her, and they kept her busy. One day one of them escaped from his cage, flew around the room, and somehow broke his leg. My wife took the bird to a veterinarian, who said he could do nothing with it. Since Jenny did not want to destroy the canary, she set the broken leg with a toothpick and some adhesive tape. Then she gave the bird a drink of cognac. In a few days the leg was as good as new.

Although business had been very good in the old place, that was not the case in the new one, not for a long time. Many of our old customers came to see us, but not as many as we expected. I remember evening after evening when there were only five people in the dining room—my wife, the faithful Carlo, Ward Morehouse (writing his column, as always), and Miriam Hopkins. Renee read books and worked crossword puzzles in her checkroom. On Friday nights Lou Schonceit, the ticket broker who had his offices next door, would bring in a small party of friends after the fights; we would put out a turkey and open some wine, but that was the only regular party we had for a long time. I began to believe that I had bitten off more than I could chew. Several times, that first summer, I considered giving it up. If it had not been for my good friend John Cerruti, I might have done it, too. Somehow, he heard that I was in trouble; without any ado, he came to me and offered to help. The only question he asked was, "How much do you need?" If it had not been for John, and for the waiters who were content to wait several months for their wages, Sardi's might have died soon after it was born.

Ward Morehouse helped us considerably, too. He mentioned the restaurant in his column five or six times a week, and I suppose he did as much as anybody to make Sardi's famous. Then other newspapermen began making their headquarters in our place. Among them was Walter Winchell, who was just beginning to establish himself as a national figure. Morehouse recalls the time that Winchell arrived and showed his friends a check for $1,000—a week's salary. Previously none of them had believed he was getting that much. "When we saw the proof, we were sick," Morehouse says. Winchell used to bring his wife and daughter in with him, sometimes two and three times a week; nobody could have been a better friend. Thanks to the items he printed about Sardi's, people began coming from all over the United States. Once a man who had no right to use the name opened a place and called it Sardi's. When Winchell heard about it, he wrote an indignant piece. I was always very grateful for that.

Winchell was a member of a group that began meeting regularly every day at lunchtime. This group called itself the Cheese Club, and consisted of reporters, free-lance writers, press agents, critics, advertising men, a photographer or two, and occasionally actors and agents. The most faithful members were Irving Hoffman, who was then working as a cartoonist; Kelcey Allen, of *Women's Wear Daily*; Louis Sobol, who was just getting started as a columnist; Sidney Skolsky, who has since become a Hollywood reporter; Mark Hellinger, then a newspaperman and later a movie producer; Richard Maney, Nat Dorfman, Marc Lachman, and several other press agents; Julius Colby, of *Variety*; Whitney Bolton, Bide Dudley, and Heywood Broun, representing the press; Jules Ziegler, an agent; Larry Wiener, an advertising man; Julius Tannen, the comic; Leonard Gallagher, stage manager and producer; and every now and then, when they were in town, George Jessel and Georgie Price. Some days there would be five or six Cheese Club members at their regular round table; other days twenty would show up. The only requirement for membership was to attend a "meeting" every now and then.

The principal function of the Cheese Club members was to provide laughs for each other, but every now and again they set to work on some constructive project. For example, there was an actress, a very attractive girl, who needed work. The club members decided that they would make her famous. Items began appearing in columns all over town, testifying to the charm and talent of the girl. The boys dropped her name everywhere. Before long an agent sold her to a producer for a big part. The girl was well on her way to stardom when, unfortunately, some of the members began getting a bit too attentive—or so some of the other members thought. The cooperative effort dissolved at once, and the girl never did become a star.

Another Cheese Club venture of this kind turned out to be a real break for the subject. Leslie Howard was looking for an actor to appear with him in *The Petrified Forest*. The

Cheese Club members heard about this and suggested a young fellow named William Gargan, who was in our place nearly every day.

"He's not well enough known," Howard said.

That was all the boys needed. They immediately began giving Gargan the same treatment the girl had received. His name appeared in all the columns. Favorable reports of his ability turned up everywhere. Lewis Milestone, the movie director, was reported to be very much interested in him as a possibility for pictures. Young Bill was famous overnight and got the part.

I was reminded of this story by Jules Ziegler, the agent, who at that time was working in the office of "Doctor" Louis Shurr, one of the most successful agents of all time. The Doctor came into the place every now and again, too, and sat with the Cheese Club. One day word came to us that he had been arrested the night before. The details of the story gave everyone a great laugh. Shurr was the man who, for years, owned a fur coat which he would allow girl friends to wear while they were out with him. At the end of the date he would take the coat back home with him, so as to allow the next evening's girl to wear it. Girl after girl schemed, planned, and connived to make Shurr hand over the coat as a present, but nobody had ever managed to get it. Well, one night he had an engagement with a girl who lived around the corner from his apartment. When he took her home, he dismissed his chauffeur. He bade the girl good night, took the coat, tossed it over his arm, and started to walk around the corner to his own place. Before he knew what was happening, a prowl-car policeman stopped him and took him to headquarters, booking him on suspicion of stealing a coat. The Doctor took a terrible kidding from Cheese Club members for weeks after that.

As I recall, the boys were never satisfied unless they were up to some practical joke, usually a cruel one. There was the time when Irving Strauss, press agent for Vincent Lopez, the orchestra leader, arranged for a girl to throw herself in the lake in Central Park, presumably out of unrequited love. The story broke everywhere. Even the *Times* carried it. Strauss' reputation as an imaginative press agent was made. This was too much for his Cheese Club friends. They hired Loring Smith, the actor, to impersonate a detective and to wait in our place until Strauss came in. When the press agent was confronted by the phony cop, he hastily left town and was not seen for a long time.

Many of the Cheese Club jokes were directed towards Kelcey Allen, the *Women's Wear* critic, one of the most faithful members of the group. Kelcey was a good-natured, innocent fellow, which made him a perfect target. One joke, I remember, kept him upset for days. It happened in the late twenties. Just after Lindbergh had flown the Atlantic in "The Spirit of St. Louis," everybody was very aviation-conscious. One day a tall, distinguished-looking Italian came into our place, and we learned that he was a flyer who was planning to duplicate Lindbergh's feat. Because of the great interest in flying, he became the focus of many stories and speculations. He seemed to like our place and began coming in every day, often with a girl much younger than he, said to be his daughter. He was an imposing man, very stern and commanding in appearance; he wanted everything just so (I remember that his waiter always had to dip his dessert apple in hot water in order to get it at the temperature he demanded). He wore a black spade beard, which added to his impressive appearance. When Kelcey Allen first saw the aviator, he asked Marc Lachman who he was.

Marc loved to tease Kelcey. "Why," he said, "that man is an experienced Italian duelist."

Kelcey said, "You mean he's killed people?"

"Several," said Marc, winking at the other Cheese Clubbers. "He's very well known in Italy."

Kelcey thought this over. He studied the man for a moment. At the time, I ought to explain right here, there was a barber's strike on in New York. "Well," Kelcey said, "he may be a big shot in Italy, but he can't even get a shave over here."

At this, the big man whirled and looked directly at Kelcey, as though he had heard.

"Uh-oh, Kelcey, now you're in for it," Marc said. "I told you he's a dangerous man! Now you've insulted him!"

Kelcey was so frightened that he stopped eating. He didn't know what to do. Finally he got up quickly, paid his check, and left as though he had an important engagement. For the next few days, Lachman and the others kidded him without mercy; since he didn't dare come into our place, they would call him at his office and tell him that the big Italian with the beard was lying in wait for him. The following week Kelcey finally ventured in. By this time he was beginning to realize that it was a joke. He sat down at a table facing the door and said, "Vincent, is it true that that man heard what I said?"

"I don't know," I said, trying to keep a straight face.

At that very moment the Italian came in. Kelcey leaped up and said to him, "I tell you, Mister, this is how it was— I was talking about the barber strike, not about you. I didn't say anything about your beard! You have a nice beard, and—"

The man turned to me and said, in Italian, "What does this man want?"

"What is he saying?" Kelcey asked me, anxiously, with one eye on the door. He was ready to make a run for it.

Truthfully, I didn't quite understand everything the big man was saying; he spoke a dialect that was different from mine. And I couldn't keep my face straight any longer.

"He doesn't understand a word of English," I told Kelcey.

Kelcey thereupon jumped up, grabbed the man's hand, and shook it, puzzling him even more. Then he went and took his regular seat at the Cheese Club table. When the other regulars came in, he pretended to them that he had seen through the joke all along. Later I heard him tell the story over and over, and each time he seemed to enjoy it as much as if it had happened to somebody else. But one day Mark Hellinger came in wearing a false beard. He sneaked up behind Kelcey, touched him on the shoulder, and said, "Booh!" Kelcey turned white.

It always seemed to me that when the Cheese Clubbers weren't playing practical jokes, they were plaguing me by bringing animals into the place. One day it was a donkey, another time a cow, another time a sea lion (Carlo fed him smelts while the newsreel cameras ground away). Ted Healy came in one day with an orangutan, and it sat down and ate lunch just like a human being. Those were not the only animal guests we had. Many, many actresses brought their dogs. Xavier Cugat showed up one time with a tiny Mexican hairless in one pocket of his coat. Romaine Simmons, the dance director for the Shuberts, sometimes came into the lobby leading a pet lion cub.

The Cheese Club survived about five years, and gradually broke up as the members became more successful or drifted into other jobs or went to Hollywood. Several of them continued to come in, however, and we often had good times as we recalled those old days. Then a new group of columnists and newspapermen came along—Ed Sullivan, Earl Wilson, Dorothy Kilgallen, Danton Walker, Robert Sylvester, Lee Mortimer, Hy Gardner, to mention only a few. They have all been very nice to Sardi's, over the years. But somehow, a person remembers the old days best. One of the most touching moments Jenny and I ever had came on the day of our Silver Wedding Anniversary. The first present we opened bore a card that said, "From the Cheese Club."

The Cheese Club and the Little Bar Fraternity were not the only clubs to organize and meet in Sardi's. One day a man named Freddie Benham came to me with a proposition. I knew him slightly; I had seen him several times with some of the Cheese Club regulars, and I had heard that he was a reporter on the *World*. Some time before, he had written a

story about the "forgotten men" of the circus. It had pro-
voked such a response that he and some friends had resolved
to set up a home where old circus men could retire and live
out their days in peace. In order to set up this home, Benham (his full name, by the way, was Frederick Darius
Benham) was forming a club to be called "The Circus Saints
and Sinners." (Years before, in Chicago, Eugene Field, the
reporter who became known for his children's poems, had
set up a club of writers called "Saints and Sinners.") Benham
and a friend of his, Chalmers L. Pancoast, had written a
draft of the club's constitution at lunch at our place one day,
and they decided that our upstairs dining room would be a
good place to eat. The New York chapter, the first of many
throughout the nation, was to be called the Dexter Fellows
Tent, after the famous press agent for Ringling Brothers
Circus. After listening to the plan, I told Benham that it
would be all right with me if the club wanted to meet in
Sardi's.

The first meeting was in 1931. The guest of honor—or
"Fall Guy"—was Count Felix von Luckner, the German
submarine commander, about whom Lowell Thomas had
written a book at the time. Actually, a guest of honor was
honored in a questionable way. He had to submit to all kinds
of indignities and to listen to the assembled guests make fun
of him. The members included men from all walks of life—
business, professional, and the entertainment world; in short,
anybody who loved the circus or just loved having a good
time with a good bunch of fellows. We erected a real tent,
and the Circus Saints and Sinners met in our place until the
group grew so large they had to find a place that offered
more room. A very good friend, Courtney Ryley Cooper, the
writer, was active in the formation of the club. I remember
him particularly because he was the first to bring J. Edgar
Hoover, the chief of the FBI, into Sardi's.

Still another group was organized in Sardi's just a few
years ago. Mayor William O'Dwyer had called for an investi-

gation of theater-ticket scalping, and Commissioner of Investigation John M. Murtagh began to make an inquiry.
Many legitimate ticket brokers around town felt they had to
band together for self-protection; they felt that such an investigation of scalpers might easily damage them in the mind
of the public. Jesse Moss, a young attorney who represents
the brokers, got Lou Schonceit and representatives of other
legitimate agencies, and together they made plans in Sardi's
to keep their good names clear. Fortunately, none of the
legitimate businessmen were hurt in the course of Murtagh's
investigation, and a good many unscrupulous operators were
driven out of business, at least temporarily.

As usual, I have been getting a little ahead of my story
and mixing up the time sequences. As I said a while back,
the Cheese Club members, especially the newspapermen,
helped business in the new place a great deal. But if credit
can be given one individual for making Sardi's as popular
as it later became, it must go to Maurice Evans. The year
was 1938—nearly eleven years after we opened. The production that caused the rush was *Hamlet*. There had been many
fine *Hamlet* performances in New York before. John Barrymore had done it, under the sponsorship of Arthur Hopkins;
and during the 1936–37 season there had been two productions running simultaneously—John Gielgud's at the Empire,
and Leslie Howard's at the Imperial. But until Maurice
Evans tried it, nobody had ever dared do the "entirety"
Hamlet in New York. Evans opened the production at the
St. James; the curtain went up at six-thirty P.M. and came
down at eleven-fifteen. (Margaret Webster directed, by the
way.) In the program there was a recommendation for Sardi's,
telling people that we served a special supper for the *Hamlet*
patrons. That seemed to do the trick. From that time on, we
began to get theatergoers as well as the players themselves.

"You see?" my wife said, when the people began rushing
us. "Glad you stayed here now, aren't you?"

She was referring to something I'd almost done when talk-

ing pictures first came in. Before *The Jazz Singer,* with Al
Jolson, had awakened the country to the fact that pictures
could speak, stage actors had had a fairly difficult time get-
ting jobs in Hollywood. All of a sudden they were in demand out there. They began leaving for the coast in droves.
It seemed to me that all our customers, even the most faithful, were rushing away—not only actors and actresses, but
producers and directors, too. (Later, George S. Kaufman and
Moss Hart wrote a play about that mad dash. They called it
Once in a Lifetime, and Sam H. Harris produced it at the
Music Box in September, 1930, with Hugh O'Connell, Jean
Dixon, and Grant Mills. It was a comedy-satire, but what
made it so good was that it was all true.) Well, I was worried.
Business was bad enough—and now this! Letters began ar-
riving from our friends who had gone to Hollywood. They
begged us to go out and start a restaurant. There was one in
the mail every day or so.

"Maybe we should go," I said to my wife.

"No," she said, firmly. "We should stay here. This is our
home."

"Maybe I should go, then, and try it for a while—and you
can stay and run this place," I suggested.

She did not even answer; she just gave me a look. It might
have been that she was opposed to my going out because,
well, she knew what happened to some men in Hollywood!
I don't know what her reasons were. All I know is that her
good sense prevailed, as it always did. It would have been a
mistake to leave New York. For, even though we gradually
began to prosper in the new place, and even though Maurice
Evans' program recommendation brought us new customers,
the family atmosphere in Sardi's remained the same, and the
place seemed more like a home than a restaurant. New York
and 44th Street—that was our neighborhood. We would have
been out of place anywhere else.

CHAPTER TEN

Cuff Customers and Con Men

ACCORDING TO THE POPULAR VIEW, actors are people who live in another world. They are not like the rest of us. They are artistic—and because they are, they are irrepressible, irresponsible and, most of the time, broke. This is the popular conception. It isn't mine. My experience with actors has been limited to those I knew in London, those I took care of in New York, and my brother Domenico; and while I knew some who lived up to that popular conception, it certainly did not apply to the majority of them. If it had, I would have been bankrupt!

It is true that I was stung many times. I carried some hopeful people for years, watching them wait around for big breaks that never came. Some of them I saw die broke. And I had the unhappy experience of watching a few—a very, very few—live off me for a time, becoming successful, and then forgetting how they'd been treated in Sardi's. There was a comic, a man who played servant parts, who was down on his luck for months. He did a lot of drinking, and he would often forget to show up for auditions when he was called. Sometimes he would feel that parts were beneath him. Other times he would say, for no good reason that I could see, "I'm not interested." I liked the fellow. I had seen him in a show or two; I thought he was talented and charming, and that it would only be a matter of time before he became as successful as he deserved to be. I fed him, his wife, and mother for two months. "You're crazy," one of the waiters said to me. I didn't think so; I had faith in him. "He'll pull himself together, wait and see," I always said. Sure enough, he did. He signed a contract with an agent who was interested in him, went out to Hollywood and began making money in the movies. He was very successful there, and became famous in a small way. I wish I could finish this story by saying that he repaid me as soon as he was able to. The truth is that although I've seen him often, I've never seen the money. I know he hasn't forgotten those months because he always mentions them when we meet. "Ah, those were the days," he says. Maybe he would pay if I pressed him, but I've never liked to dun a man and I have no intention of beginning this late in life.

There were others who stuck me. An old-time character actor, a man I'd known from the Bartholdi Inn days, was heavily in debt and couldn't get a job on the New York stage. One day a producer I knew came in. He told me he was looking for a certain type of actor, and I thought of my old Bartholdi Inn friend. I introduced them. The producer gave him the part, and everything was fine—until the show closed. My old friend, who had not paid all his debts, was still short of ready cash. He told me he thought he might be able to do some work in Hollywood. I advanced him fare and some pocket money, and he went out to the coast and began working regularly. I never heard from him. A few years later, when my wife and I were out there, we called him up and invited him to dinner. He was doing very well, he said. He made that clear. He didn't mention the money he owed the restaurant—but, as usual, he graciously permitted me to pick up the check for our reunion dinner.

It happened sometimes that an actor whom I regarded as

a good risk would run up a bill of three or four hundred dollars and then disappear without warning. It was funny, in a way. He'd be in the place day after day, eating lunch and dinner there, turning up for the cocktail hour, getting messages from Felix and Jimmy and Carlo, leaving messages for others, sometimes using the telephone, joking with Oreste the bartender, flirting with the hat-check girl—and then, like a flash, he would vanish off the face of the earth as far as Sardi's was concerned. Many actors did this to me. If they had come and said, "Sardi, I am out of work now—I'll pay when I get a job," I would have carried them indefinitely. Sometimes I carried them even when they didn't say that, because I knew I would get it back sooner or later. But the ones that just disappeared—well, I used to get furious. Sometimes I would swear never to trust an actor again. But then my wife would remind me how much I owed to honest people in the theater, and I would calm down. Well, I thought, if you lose your faith in human nature, you lose everything. So I went on permitting them to charge. When Cino took over the place at the time I retired, he and John Brasi threw out a three-foot drawer full of unpaid checks. I'd forgotten all about them.

But I want to emphasize again that it frequently happened that my faith in human beings was rewarded. Actors I hadn't seen for years would arrive, hand me a roll of bills, and say, "Here, I owe you this." Even today, people sometimes give money to Cino in payment for bills they ran up in my day.

The truth is that as far as that popular conception of actors is concerned, most actors are not very good actors. They don't play the part the way it's written. When James Cagney was a youngster—he was a hoofer then—he spent a lot of time in our place. He was a thin, nervous boy, always on the go, always restless for the break he knew was coming. Long after he became a star in films, he stopped in one day with his manager. He called me over to their table and said, "In the old days, when I was trying to get chorus boy parts, there were a good many times when all I had to eat in twenty-four hours was a bowl of Sardi's soup—on credit!" Ted Healy, always a very good friend of mine, went nearly a year without paying; I always knew that I would get it, and sure enough, I did.

My favorite story is about José Ferrer. He tells it himself, so I don't imagine he'll mind if I do. After he had done so well in *Charley's Aunt* in 1940 and as Iago in *Othello* in 1943, he was out of work for a long time. That sometimes happens in the theater; even some of the biggest names do not keep busy all the time. I know one topnotch actress whose last play was a great personal triumph; that was four years ago, and she has not worked since. But, anyhow, Ferrer kept signing checks in our place. One day he looked at the total. It was over $1,200. "Well," he said, "I guess I'll simply have to get to work." He decided that he would do the first show that came along. Shortly after that he picked up a copy of *Cyrano*. Today he tells people that he never would have won the Academy Award if it hadn't been for the bill he owed Sardi's!

I can't explain, exactly, how I knew which people to trust and which to doubt. I suppose the days as a head waiter must have taught me something about reading a man's character by glancing at his face. Shortly after Sardi's moved from its original location into its present one, a man named John Clark came strolling in one fine spring evening. He was an executive with Paramount Pictures and had eaten with us a few times at lunch, but that was all I knew about him. He didn't waste any time in telling me what he wanted.

"Hey, Sardi," he said, "I'm staying in town tonight and I need cash—give me a hundred."

He had an honest face, and I gave it to him immediately, although it took everything in the register right down to the dollar bills. Clark turned to a man who was with him and said, "Look at the poor sucker—he hardly knows me, but he gives me a hundred bucks, even though it cleans him out!"

The first thing in the morning, he walked in and handed me a crisp new $100 bill—as I had known he would. From then on, he ate at our place every day, always at the same table, and always with a big party. He constantly talked about the place to other people in the movie business, and before long the men from Warner Brothers, M-G-M, and the rest of the movie companies were turning up almost as regularly. One day he broke his glasses at lunch. I saw it happen, and mentioned that I happened to have a nephew, an oculist, who occupied a suite in a building nearby. I had the glasses fixed while he was eating. Later he bought an Italian-style home in the country and wanted to have it redecorated. He asked me if I knew of an architect who knew anything about Italian design. My daughter, Anna, was then being courted by the young man whom she later married— Frank Gina. He at that time was studying architecture. When I told this to Mr. Clark, he laughed and said, "My God, can't I do *anything* without having a Sardi mixed up in it in some way?" But he gave the commission to the son-in-law-to-be. It was the boy's first job and started him on a successful career. All of which, I suppose, goes to show what trusting your instincts about people will do for you.

One day a tall blonde girl with a pointed chin and big eyes came up to me as I was standing near the entrance and gave me a story I'd heard nearly a hundred times. She explained that she was trying to get on the stage and didn't know a soul in New York; she was expecting a check from her parents which probably would arrive within a week or two, but meanwhile she had no money for food. She seemed sincere, and she did have a nice face. "Well, I can't let you starve," I said, and put her at a table. She came in the next night, and the next, and in fact nearly every night from then on. Finally, to my surprise, she did show me a check from her parents. I cashed it for her, and she paid her bill.

She continued to eat with us and became a good friend, and
eventually she went on to earn a fantastic salary as a singer,
comedienne, and actress on the stage, in the movies, and in
night clubs. Her name is Celeste Holm. We still see her in
the place whenever she is in New York.

While I always fed anybody who was hungry and honestly
couldn't pay—after all, I'd been down and out many times
in my younger days—I never gave food away free in exchange
for publicity, as so many of my fellow restaurateurs did and
do. Yet most of the newspapermen continued to come in
and give me much free news space, particularly those in the
Cheese Club. Once when I was hoping to get some new business a friend told me I ought to hire a press agent, so I
agreed to give it a try. The experiment didn't work out too
well. I agreed that the press agent and his guests would not
have to pay for their food; he was simply to sign the tab and
give it to a waiter. Later I learned that he was not only signing the tab, but also collecting from his guests outside! That
was the end of our arrangement.

In all my years, there was only one person who never received a check: John Golden. The reason was very simple.
Mr. Golden did not want to see his tab. He asked that the
waiter keep it, add whatever he deemed a reasonable tip,
and turn it over to the cashier. At the end of each month, he
would send his secretary with a check to cover his charges.

Not all theatrical people are as businesslike as Mr. Golden,
of course, but it seems to me that for the most part, they've
undergone a metamorphosis during the the past forty years.
Today there don't seem to be as many irresponsibles as there
once were. Even those who formerly had an easy-come, easy-
go attitude are settling down, raising families, even going
into business on the side. There never was a man who enjoyed life more than James Barton, the old vaudeville headliner, known for his drunk act and soft-shoe routines. He is
now in his sixties and still going strong, as he proved in 1951
when he opened on Broadway as the star of *Paint Your*

Wagon. Some years ago, he and his wife bought themselves a bar-and-grill along one of the turnpikes on Long Island. Gloria Swanson, the epitome of feminine glamour, is interested financially in several manufacturing concerns, among them a tool-and-die company. Walter Abel has real estate holdings; Alfred Drake and others have been Wall Street investors for years. William Gaxton is in the men's toiletries business; Morton Downey is active on the board of a soft-drink manufacturing company. Bing Crosby's many business enterprises include a race track, an interest in a baseball club, and numerous inventions. Frederic March has an interest in a California company that manufactures recording tape. Milton Berle, at this writing, is a big investor in a Broadway restaurant. And I could go on like this indefinitely. When I take the train into New York from my home in Manhasset, Long Island, I often run into Dennis King, the former matinee idol who is still very active on the stage, and Harry McNaughton, the English comic who was a part of Phil Baker's retinue for many years and who now works in television. Do they talk about things that they've seen in *Variety?* They do not. They discuss investments, securities, annuities, etc., sounding for all the world like a couple of bankers.

Although several actors in my acquaintance were careless, thoughtless, and unreliable, I can't remember a single instance in which an actor or anyone connected with the stage deliberately set out to swindle me. Wait—there was one. A member of a very well-known producing family beat the restaurant out of $287 by giving us checks on a company that he later claimed—when the time came to cash them— was no longer in business. But since that man was not really an actor, I don't hold it against the profession. Our hat-check girls sometimes complained that many famous personages slipped them slugs, buttons, and worthless medallions, but I never saw any proof of that.

On the other hand, I fell more than once for hoaxes carried out by professional thieves. Some of them were so simple

I never should have been caught; others were more compli-
cated. But I wasn't always Sardi the Sucker; I saw through
their games many times, too. It was common practice for
some thieves to declare that they were relatives of good customers of mine, but I'm sad to say that there were some
honest-to-goodness relatives who were also honest-to-goodness thieves. One, the brother of a well-known actor, still
owes me nearly $500.

The swindles that angered me most, I suppose, were those
involving close friends of mine. Edmund Gwenn was an old
customer of ours, dating back to the first Sardi's. Whenever
he came to town, he ate with us every day. One year while
appearing in a play on 45th Street he had to go on a strict
diet, which we followed closely in preparing his food. On
matinee days we used to send him a tray over between performances, so that he would not have to leave his dressing
room. One day we sent Gwenn his tray as usual, but the boy
who had delivered it had no sooner returned to the restaurant
when the telephone rang.

"This is Mr. Gwenn's valet," said a voice. "Mr. Gwenn
has a guest. He wishes you to send another tray—and change
for $20."

As the boy was going through Shubert Alley on his second
trip, a man stopped him and announced himself as the valet.
"I've got to go to the drugstore for Mr. Gwenn," he said.
"Give me the change you brought—Mr. Gwenn will give you
the twenty."

When the boy got to the dressing room, he found the real
valet there. No second dinner had ever been ordered. We
were never certain who did it.

One quiet evening when we were still in the old location,
Carlo and I were sitting by the cigar showcase in front when
the door suddenly opened and a boy rushed in, very excited.
"Hide me, hide me!" he cried. "The police are after me!
Hide me, please!"

The boy was about twenty, not badly dressed. He looked

as though he might have come from a good family. The story
he told didn't make much sense. He said he was from Philadelphia, where his father was in the restaurant business. His
father had often mentioned me as a kind man, he said, and
now that he was in trouble he was looking to me for assistance. I didn't recognize his father's name, but I thought
I might have met him somewhere or other. Then I asked the
boy what sort of trouble he was in.

"I came to New York and spent all my money, and then I
did a foolish thing that got the police after me," he said. "If
my father finds out, he'll kill me."

His need was not great. All he wanted was $5 to get back
to Philadelphia, and when he got there he would have his
father send me a check immediately. I didn't like the idea
of a boy his age going to jail, so I gave it to him.

Well, I never heard from the fictitious father, but I saw
the boy once again. It happened about two years after we
moved from the old to the new place. Again it was a quiet
evening. I was standing by the cash register in the rear when
he appeared. His face was familiar, but I couldn't place him
at first—not until he began going through the same story,
almost word for word. Before he got to the part about not
wanting his father to find out, I interrupted and finished
the story for him. The look on his face was something to see!
He jumped up like a policeman in a Mack Sennett movie
and went through the front door like lightning.

Some detectives once told me that such swindle artists
work the restaurants methodically, and that when they've
finished with a list of places they start all over and go through
it a second time. I had experiences with two other men who
did just that. One morning a very well-dressed man who
spoke good Italian came in and asked for me. He said he
lived in the Bronx and had come downtown to pick up a
cablegram that had arrived from his mother in the old country. He wanted to cable her an answer, but he'd left his
money at home. The cable cost a dollar, and all he had was

twenty cents. He spoke so convincingly that I gave him not only the dollar but also carfare home. He promised to bring the money back the next day. He never showed up. Later, another restaurant man told me he had been taken with the same story.

One cold December night I stepped outside for some air just before the arrival of the supper crowd. A man was standing in front of the place with a child in his arms. He was not dressed warmly and he appeared miserable, but he said nothing to me; he merely stood there, watching the crowds, with a lost, wistful expression on his face. Finally my curiosity got the better of me, and I asked if there was anything the matter.

He replied in French. He had been working up the street at Hotel Astor as a cook, but he had quit the job to take one he had been offered in Baltimore. His wife was dead, and he wanted to go to Baltimore because he thought the climate would be better for the child. Also, if he didn't take the child with him, the authorities would take it away from him. He said all this very simply, with dignity.

"How are you going to get to Baltimore?" I asked.

"I'm hitchhiking," he said. He didn't explain how he hoped to hitch a ride to Baltimore from the middle of 44th Street, but by then I was so concerned I didn't think to ask for an explanation. He said that he and the child had had no dinner, so I took him into the place, put him at a table, and told him to order whatever he wanted.

Now, most of my customers, having known hard times themselves, are always willing to help someone else who needs it. They may complain about taxes, the high cost of living, and the rest of the things that irritate all of us, but when it comes to giving a helping hand, they are always first in line. James Montgomery Flagg, the artist, was sitting with some friends, as he used to nearly every night. When he saw the man and the child, he couldn't resist asking about them. He was so touched by the story as I repeated it that he went around from table to table and put the bite on the other customers. His collection came to more than $20. When I gave it to the man he accepted it gravely. Tears came into his eyes. Then he left, still carrying the child.

A few days later, I was surprised to see the same man doing the same thing, except this time he and the child were standing in front of a restaurant in Times Square. I went right up to him and said, "What, didn't you go to Baltimore?"

"Oh," he said, "excuse me, excuse me, excuse me," and hurried away. I didn't have the heart to tell Jim Flagg how we'd been taken.

Some swindlers went to extraordinary lengths to pull their games. Twenty years or more ago, I came into the restaurant one morning and found my wife and John Brasi waiting for me at a table with a stranger. Both seemed excited. "Oh, Vincent," my wife said, "we're going to have a wonderful party here! Talk to this gentleman, please!"

The man said he was a representative of an Italian company that controlled some coffee plantations in Brazil. He said that it had been the custom of his company for many years to send half its staff to England for a Christmas holiday. While in England, the people always ate at Pagani's; since the company footed the bills, they ate nothing but the best. The last night of the vacation there was always a champagne party with all the extras. This year the program had been changed. The company was planning to send its staff to New York instead of London, and my restaurant had been chosen tentatively as the dining headquarters. Price was absolutely no object, but everything would have to be letter-perfect. First, could I cook Italian style? (I should have become suspicious then and there!) Second, would he get my assurance that every meal would be different? To prove that we could do the job, I took him on a personal tour of the restaurant, into the kitchen, upstairs to the party room, letting him examine the china and silverware, urging him to sample dishes that were being prepared. He seemed pleased.

Back at the table, he began dictating menus to Brasi. He must have spent a half hour or more at it. We were ready to shake hands and call it a deal when I asked him how soon he would be returning to Brazil.

"Very soon," he said, "as soon as I can get a certain small difficulty straightened out."

That was when he made his pitch, but I was too eager for the business to suspect anything. He said that he'd made many purchases in England before coming to New York, among them twelve cases of carbon paper. For some reason which he didn't bother to explain, he'd only declared eleven of the twelve cases when he stopped off in New York. The twelfth had been confiscated. He didn't say who had confiscated it, or why, or how he could sell it, but he said he had to get rid of it. He snapped his fingers as though he'd just had a brilliant idea.

"Mr. Sardi," he said, casually, "why don't you buy the carbon paper from me now?" His voice became confidential. "Then you could put it on the bill you send my company for the party. I would appreciate it a lot—it would save me some embarrassment."

"What would I do with a case of carbon paper?" I asked. "I don't even have a typewriter. My wife and Brasi, here, do all our office work by hand."

"Maybe you could distribute it among your friends or sell it," he said, reasonably.

At that moment, Brasi, who had been staring at the man, jumped up in excitement. "Hey!" he cried, "I know you! You the crook!"

Before coming to work with us, Brasi had been employed in another restaurant owned by a friend of mine. Three years before, the same man had come in there with the same story.

When Brasi began yelling, the man scrambled to his feet, gathered his papers together and streaked for the door. I started to chase him, but he had too much of a start; by the

time I got to the door, he was halfway down the block. My
wife was so disappointed she nearly cried. Brasi and I just
smiled at each other and shook hands.

Not every con man went to such elaborate devices. One
group got some money from me by declaring that they were
collecting for a Christmas tree to be put up in Times Square.
Another said they were collecting funds for the election cam-
paign of a phony judge.

The worst experience I ever had was the time I was taken
by a man I have since come to think of as the meanest man
I ever knew. I have already told how, when we moved into
our new location, business was terrible, at first. Now that I
was the owner of a bigger, more elaborate establishment I
had to compete with my nearest comparable neighbor, the
Hotel Astor, up at the corner of 44th and Broadway. That
meant I had to make the menus more varied and raise my
old prices. When I did that, we lost some of our old trade.
I had a gold coin that I carried for luck in those days, a
twenty-dollar gold piece. Each evening, as I stood by the door
waiting for customers, I flipped the coin; I liked to think that
if it came up heads, business would be good. Once, when I
flipped it, it fell into Barbara Stanwyck's soup—but even that
didn't improve business. (Miss Stanwyck didn't mind; she
was dining with Frank Fay, whom she later married.) Finally
I had to use the coin for current expenses. I substituted a
silver dollar, but soon I couldn't even afford that. At one
point business was so terrible I sank to flipping a quarter.
It was around that time that a man came in and raised my
spirits immensely.

He was a man who walked with a limp, a food-checker
I'd known at the Palais Royale. I always had thought of him
as a nice fellow, and I was glad to see him. When he asked
how I was doing, I told him the truth.

"I have a party for you that might help," he said. "Right
now I am food buyer for the two biggest hospitals in New
Jersey. The nurses at one of them are having a theater party

this week, and they want to have lunch beforehand. I'll suggest your place to them."

I asked if they would want the seventy-five-cent lunch or the dollar one.

"Oh, this has got to be much more elaborate than that," he answered. "I want you to order everything special, and make it a $2.50 lunch, at least."

In those days—the mid-thirties—that was a high price for a lunch. Together, then, he and I planned the menu. We were to have celery and olives, oysters, lamb chops, peas, potato, green salad, dessert, and coffee. The food was to be ready and waiting on the table when the nurses arrived, he specified, and then he left, promising to return the next day. Sure enough, he came back and said that the nurses were delighted with the meal we had planned; but he emphasized again that the food would have to be ready and waiting on the table. As he was about to leave he pointed at a box of cigars in the glass case by the register and said he wanted three of them. I was so grateful to him for bringing me this fine party I was ready to give him the box, but he said he wanted only three, and he insisted on paying. Then he discovered that he had no money, and asked if I would cash a ten-dollar check. I cashed it willingly and again tried to press the cigars on him, but again he refused.

Next day, everything was in readiness. We had bought the food especially, cooked it as ordered, shined the silver, and put out the best china. Twelve-thirty came, but the nurses didn't. Nor were they there by one. By one-thirty I realized the truth. The miserable creature had gone to all that trouble simply to cash a ten-dollar check—which I would have cashed anyhow, on the strength of our former acquaintance! I was stuck with all that food we'd bought and prepared, not to mention the check, which came back a few days later. That's one man I've been looking for ever since.

Marc Lachman, the press agent, once played a joke of a similar nature on me, but not with the same disastrous results. Marc always loved jokes, and one day he went into a telephone booth in the restaurant and dialed the number of our house phone, disguising his voice.

"Mr. Sardi, I am bringing two hundred Boy Scouts over for lunch," he said.

"Fine. What day, please?"

"What day? Today, of course!"

"How soon?"

"Within the hour!"

Such scurrying around as went on! I thought George, who was then head waiter, would lose his mind as he tore upstairs and started clearing the big room to handle the party. Marc had ordered chicken on the telephone, so I began making frantic calls to butchers to locate enough for two hundred lunches. All this time Marc and his friends were sitting at a nearby table, watching the commotion and laughing as though it were the funniest thing they'd ever seen. But they didn't have the heart to let the joke go on. They finally told us—but we heard about Boy Scouts for weeks thereafter.

Shortly after that I was caught on one of the oldest con games known, the one called "Breaking the Note." The way I was caught was particularly embarrassing. When our Little Bar was located next to the front entrance, the bartender, then a German who could scarcely speak English, was having his lunch one day when a man walked in and asked for change for a $20 bill. When the bartender gave it to him, the man said, "Wait—I see I did have the right change, after all. Give me back the twenty." The bartender complied, but he did not, as the man had hoped, forget to ask for the return of the change he had handed over. I'll say one thing for that con man: he was persistent. He marched right out of the Little Bar and went to the cash register, where I was standing. I gave him change for the twenty, chatted a few minutes, and then, when he wanted the twenty back, completely forgot to get my change! My wife had a few things to say about that later, you can be sure. "Imagine," she said, "a man who couldn't speak English saw through the scheme—and you fell for it!" The fellow later was caught as he was trying to work the trick on a florist shop nearby.

Like most restaurant proprietors, I had my share of run-ins with people who claimed they'd found objects in their food. Those people were comparatively easy to deal with. It was the "accident victims" who were more difficult. When I had an awning marquee out front, I was continually plagued by people looking for free money. One man waited until he was certain that John Poggi, the waiter, was watching him. Then, as Poggi looked on, he deliberately tripped over one of the awning supports. He shook his fist at Poggi and said, "Tell your boss I'm going to sue!" A few days later we got a letter from the man's lawyer—that is, we thought it was from the lawyer until the insurance company's investigator found that the man had had stationery printed and had written the letter himself, hoping to get a settlement for his "injury."

From the time that my place first began to gain a reputation, I was plagued by begging letters from abroad. When I retired some newspapers mentioned it, and the story was picked up and given wide circulation in the Italian press. There it was puffed up all out of proportion. A friend over there sent me a clipping from an Italian paper that was headlined

MULTIMILLIONAIRE SARDI REFUSES TO WORK ANY LONGER

At once the letters began coming in. There must have been five or six hundred of them within a few weeks. No doubt some of them were from worthy, needy people—I always wished that I'd had some way of checking—but the majority were so strange as to be laughable. One asked for a piano. "Maybe you have one you don't want tucked off in a corner somewhere," it said. Another woman wrote and said that her father had often spoken of me: he had been very proud of the success I'd had in the United States. "Now I have a son," she continued. "He's twenty years old—just the age you were when you left Italy. In all his life he's never had a good time. Could you send $400 for my son to have a good time?" But not all the letters were from beggars; several were from playwrights, poets, novelists, musicians, and actors. One man sent me a play that had a character named Sardi in it. Clement Wood wrote a poem, "Ode to Sardi."

The strangest letter of all came from a man who thought that I might be his father. He owned a shop in Rome, he said, and for years he had been spending all his profits in an attempt to trace his parentage. All he knew about his father was that the gentleman had been courting a lady of excellent social standing and that a baby had been born of the court- ship and placed in a foundling home. The man had learned from a nurse in the home that the father had visited him as a baby, had left some English coins, and promised to send money regularly from America. The father had been born, the nurse told my "son," in 1885, and had come to the United States in 1907.

My wife read this letter. "What can it mean?" she asked.

"Well," I said, "I have to admit that the dates are right— except that at the time this baby was born, I was in the army in another part of Italy, and I'd been there for a year." And then I told her, again, one of my personal rules: "About fire and women, I've always been very careful. Both too hot!"

CHAPTER ELEVEN

Caught Off Gard

A s I have mentioned, business was very bad in the new place for months after we opened. I would stand at the front door each mealtime, flipping my coin, but even though it sometimes showed up heads, it didn't bring us luck. The customers passed us by, heading for the Hotel Astor or the Broadway restaurants. Renee Carroll was superstitious: she thought that if she came to work hungry, business would be good, but it was bad even on nights when she was ravenous. One evening when our straits were dire indeed—that was the time when I had sunk to flipping a dime—I all but decided to give up and go back to being a waiter full-time.

"I can't understand it," I said to Jenny. "Here we are in the heart of the theatrical section, a location that most restaurant owners would give anything for—and yet we've got no business. Why is it? Our food is good, our prices are reasonable, we've trained the waiters in the old tradition. Why won't people come in?"

"It may be that food and service aren't enough," my wife said. "Maybe we need something else."

I briefly considered putting in an orchestra—very briefly, because I couldn't afford to hire one. In fact, I could barely afford to keep the place open much longer.

"Maybe theatrical people would come if they felt it was *their* place," my wife said.

"I know," I said. "But we've done everything to make them feel at home, and still they don't come. What else can we do?"

"It ought to be something dramatic," my wife said.

It was then that the idea came to me. I remembered Joe Zelli's restaurant in Paris, where all the celebrities dined. Why, I wondered, did they go there? As I recalled the place, the furnishings were no better than ours; nor were the food and service. Then I thought of something else. Zelli's walls were covered with caricatures of famous people who had eaten there. That, I thought, was probably the secret. The celebrities were going to Zelli's because he put up their pictures. I told all this to my wife, and she agreed it was worth a try.

My next problem was finding an artist. The first person I thought of was Irving Hoffman, who as a member of the Cheese Club often ate lunch in our place. Irving today is one of the busiest men I know: a press agent, a magazine writer, and I do not know what all. When I first knew him, he was less successful, but he was almost as busy. And, as a matter of fact, he was extraordinarily successful for his age, which was sixteen or seventeen. He was a theatrical cartoonist, selling his sketches to newspapers and humor magazines, and something of a young man about town—he always came into the place with a pretty actress or singer, such as Ginger Rogers or Helen Morgan. He was so busy that when I approached him to do our cartoons, he had to turn me down. But he added that he knew of a man who might want the job.

One morning each week Irving and his fellow cartoonists took their wares to the theatrical editors who bought them— to Walter Winchell at the *Graphic,* Alexander Woollcott at the *World,* and Heywood Broun at the *Post.* Waiting in the reception rooms to see the editors, Irving had become friendly with a White Russian refugee, recently arrived in this country, who called himself Alex Gard. It was a strange friendship, in a way, because neither liked the other's drawings. Yet Hoffman was fair enough to know that although he himself was not an admirer of Gard's work, many other people were. When he showed me some samples, I thought they were very good. "Bring him around, and we'll make a bargain," I said.

A few days later Irving showed up with Gard in tow. The artist was a medium-sized man with darkish hair, strong features, and an accent like that of the Mad Russian on the old Eddie Cantor radio show. His eyes were as sharp as his clothes were sloppy—but although he dressed carelessly, he always walked with a stick. There was elegance about him. He seldom wore a hat (although later, after he had been coming into the place for so long that he was one of the family, Renee gave him a permanent pass to the checkroom). I explained to him what it was I wanted him to do, but he made it clear that he, too, had definite ideas on the subject. First, he wanted to select the people he would caricature. Second, he insisted that his version be accepted as final—there could be no changes in a drawing once it was finished. Third, he wanted to supply his own materials.

After I had agreed to all this, we started talking about pay. Gard astonished me by insisting that he wanted nothing but food in return for his work. Considering my own finances, I was delighted to agree.

At this point in our negotiations he drew Hoffman aside and began whispering. I found out later from Irving that he said: "How do I know this man's food vill be good?"

"The food at Sardi's is excellent," Irving reassured him.

"Vat the hell, maybe he vill cheat me to meals and give me bad food," Gard persisted.

"Draw up a contract, then," Irving suggested.

A proper legal document was prepared. It provided for all the things that Gard had asked for, and also stipulated that I was to serve him one meal a day for himself and one guest. If he by chance missed a day, he was not to be permitted to have two meals, or three guests, the day following (he missed few meals from then on until his death). The agreement also stated that I was not to criticize his drawings, and that he was not to complain about my food. With Hoffman witnessing, we signed the contract and put it in the office strongbox. Later, when we became close friends, we often joked about our contract. Today it is one of my most treasured souvenirs.

A few days thereafter Gard went out and bought fifty black frames and placed them on the walls near the entrance. As nearly as I can recall, Ted Healy was the first person he asked to pose. Gard's method of choosing a subject was simple: he drew only people he liked. This was odd, since he had an eye like a merciless camera. When he saw a person, he seemed to see only the worst features. Such a collection of long, humped, and crooked noses, bulging eyes, weak chins, buck teeth, warts, moles, and wens! At first, I must say I was worried about what the actors would think; I was sure that Gard's ugly drawings might drive some of the more sensitive ones away.

The people Gard drew all had to be connected with the theater or the arts in some way. He called them "All Gard's Chillun," or "Gard's Chosen People." Once Irving brought in Lady Viola Tree, of the celebrated English acting family, so that he could say "Only Gard can make a Tree." Gard was so selective that he at times became insulting to people he didn't want to draw. One of the Gianninis, of the West Coast banking dynasty, became a customer of ours and very much wanted to have his own picture on the wall. Gard always turned him down. "I wouldn't draw a banker for ten thousand dollars," he said. To Gard's surpise, he in turn was sometimes refused by subjects he wanted. John Golden declared that he had an allergy to having his picture placed on public exhibition—which always made me a little sad, for he was one of those I was most anxious to "honor" with a caricature. Helen Hayes held out for a long time, but later consented. Lee Shubert posed, but his brother J. J. always remained adamant.

Gard had quite an interesting background before coming to America. His real name was Alexis Kremkoff, and he was born in Kazan, Russia, into a family whose men were prominent in the Russian navy. Alex attended the Russian Naval Academy until 1917, then went to sea on a destroyer. At the time of the Russian Revolution, he and his crewmates were in Paris. When they heard what had happened, they deserted immediately. Gard bummed about Paris for a time, taking jobs where he could get them. He decorated one restaurant there, and in that way got money to come to the United States. When he first landed here he didn't get much work to do, which was one of the reasons why Irving recommended him to me. A kindhearted man, Irving knew that Alex would welcome the opportunity to eat steadily.

Sometimes, when Gard and I were sitting around talking after the dinner crowd had gone, he would tell me what he had heard of the fate of his family in Russia. Apparently they had a terrible time. His father had been an admiral in the Russian Navy, and after his death there was no one to look out for Gard's brothers and sisters, one of whom was made a political prisoner and sent off to Siberia. When Alex spoke of these matters his eyes filled with tears, and he always hoped that he might some day get back to see his relatives again. When World War II came, he enlisted in the U. S. Navy, although he was far over the age of the draft. He became a Quartermaster Second Class.

During the time I knew him, Gard never quite lost the Russian accent. He often made funny language blunders. When inviting Irving Hoffman to dine with him, he would say, "Irving, come—ve'll do dinner between ourselfs!" Another time, he told of an incident that had occurred while he was sketching a rehearsal of a Max Reinhardt play. "All of a sudden I fell down my pencil and made a hell of a noise!" he said. I always called him "Mr. Gard," and he called me "Mr. Sardi," except when he said it, it came out "Missardi."

Gard's temperament was as typically Russian as his accent. It showed plainly in the way he worked. He would sit down with the subject, scowling at him fiercely from every angle, and then, accompanied by muttered Russian oaths, he would streak his pencil across his drawing pad. It was seldom that a caricature took him more than a half hour. On this original, he always indicated his colors in lightly penciled words— in Russian, of course. Later, at home, he would make the drawing permanent in India ink, India color, and water color. After doing it once in color, he would run water in his bathtub, put the drawing in there, then dry it out and repeat the process, washing out and renewing the colors until no amount of water could have harmed them. If New York is ever hit by a tidal wave, it's reasonably certain that the Gard caricatures at Sardi's will survive. Gard used to say that they would retain their color even if they were kept at the bottom of the ocean for twenty years.

After he had done about a hundred drawings, he began getting offers from other restaurant owners. He always refused to work for them. The Brown Derby, in Hollywood, offered him a fantastic sum to go out there. "I hate Hollywood," Gard said, settling the matter. I never could understand why he stayed with us, for he could have done very well elsewhere. It was particularly odd, considering that he never earned much from his outside work. One of his books, *The Stars off Gard,* sold fairly well, and so did those he published while in the navy. He sold an occasional drawing to the magazines or newspapers, but when he died we learned that he was almost penniless. I suppose he stayed with us out of friendship and loyalty.

As I have remarked, Gard was one of the cruelest caricaturists who ever lived. He often remarked that one of his hardest subjects was Walter Winchell, whose features were so regular and even that he could find little to satirize or ridicule. (He seemed a bit wistful when he said it.) He was harder on women than on men, but as I recall, women were better sports than the men were. Since he always told his subjects that he never drew anyone except people he was fond of, it was natural for most of them to accept his savage versions of their faces good-naturedly, but there must have been some who were hurt.

Katharine Cornell was one of Gard's first subjects—perhaps the first of the women, if I am not mistaken. At the time she was in our restaurant almost every day. She and my wife were great friends, and I had devised a special salad which we named for her and featured on the menu. (Eventually we had to take it off. Miss Cornell has a passion for garlic, and most people don't like it as well as she. After ordering the salad, they would send it back.) Gard drew Miss Cornell with a cigarette drooping from her mouth, which offended her. She asked to have the cigarette taken off the picture. Gard refused. "Gard never changes or repeats himself," he said. My wife, however, stepped in and protested so indignantly that he finally made the change, snarling about meddling women. Miss Cornell is still not too fond of the drawing. When Gard drew Josephine Hull, my wife again raised such a fuss that he did the whole thing over. The new one was not much kinder, but it went up on the wall.

Gard made one other change that I recall. It was done at the behest of the late Kelcey Allen. As I have said, Kelcey was a gentle, yet excitable, soul. He was known for his humorous remarks, such as the one he made on an opening night, during intermission of a particularly bad play. As Kelcey and his fellow critics were standing on the sidewalk, a van from Cain's, the theatrical warehouse where sets are sent after a play closes, happened to pass down the street. Kelcey waved to the driver and called, "Over here! Over here!"

When Gard finished Kelcey's caricature, the critic looked it over and said, "My lips are too thick, Alex—couldn't you put in a little cigar or something?" Gard agreed, and Kelcey was very pleased. He always liked to sit at a table where he could look at his caricature, and he had a harmless vanity about it that was amusing. One day a waiter came up to me and said, "Mr. Allen wants to see you right away—says it's very important!" When I got to Kelcey's table, I found him in a state of high excitement. "Vincent," he whispered, "there's a fly sitting on the nose of my picture—would you please go and shoo it away?"

Fannie Hurst, the novelist, was eager to have Gard do her caricature, but when he finally did, she was very much put out. She thought he had made her stouter than she was. Her husband got in touch with Walter Winchell and asked him to ask me to talk to Gard about changing it. Winchell then came to me and said that Miss Hurst was interested in buying the picture. "Sorry," I said. "If Miss Hurst likes it so much, Alex might draw her a copy—but the original belongs to Sardi's."

Gard sometimes did make copies, for which he charged fifty dollars. Miss Hurst never ordered one, for some reason. Nor did many others. When Helen Morgan saw what Gard had done to her wistful face, she literally burst into tears. She refused to put her name on it, and signed it with an X. John Anderson, the critic, was another who refused to sign. Georgie Price, the comic, signed his, but when it was put up he always chose a table far away from it. Louis Sobol once asked Gard to make his picture a little less devastating, but Gard wouldn't do it. Sometime thereafter Sobol's picture disappeared. We never did learn what happened to it. To me, the most savage one Gard ever did was of Sam H. Harris, the producer, which showed him eating spaghetti in a rather disorderly fashion. Mr. Harris never seemed to mind; in fact, he thought it was funny.

Gard did all his sketches right in the restaurant except the one over the door—a big one of former Mayor Jimmy Walker. At one time the mayor was a regular customer; he would park his official car on 44th Street and drop in for coffee while waiting for Betty Compton, who was playing in a show across the street. But when Gard asked him to do his caricature, the mayor declared he was too busy to pose in Sardi's. The artist therefore went down to City Hall to do his sketch.

Several times, husbands and wives asked Gard to draw them together. He almost always refused; he was foresighted enough to know that the double drawing might embarrass the couple if, as sometimes happened, they were later separated. We compromised in some cases by hanging husband and wife side by side—and then, if the marriage fell apart, we waited a reasonable time and moved one or the other. Gard did draw a number of celebrated collaborators together, among them Rodgers and Hammerstein, and Howard Lindsay and Russel Crouse. Around the time the drawing was made, Lindsay and Crouse were at the peak of a long string of successes which included *Life with Father, State of the Union,* and their sponsorship of *Arsenic and Old Lace.* The movies were then fond of making pictures about famous show business teams, such as Rodgers and Hart. Seeing the caricatures, someone said to Buck Crouse, "Now that your picture's hanging in Sardi's, maybe the movies will do a picture about you and Howard." Crouse nodded seriously. "That's right," he said, "with Charles Coburn and C. Aubrey Smith." Ed Wynn and his son, Keenan, make up another pair on the wall just inside the entrance. On his, Keenan wrote, "It took 12 years, but at last I made it. The character next to me has talent, too."

Most of Gard's subjects tried to add a humorous or sarcastic line to their signatures. Some of them got back at him. Jean Simmons scribbled, "I *must* try to cultivate that expression." Arthur Margetson's was shorter: "If *you* say so." Georgie Price's was "Well, my mother loves me, anyhow." The late Lupe Velez, irrepressible as usual, put down, "God, but I am beautiful!" Warner Baxter lamented, "My God, what good photography can do!" Cary Grant threatened, "I'll come up and see *you* some time, too." Harold Lloyd shrugged it off. "What the hell," he wrote. Boris Karloff's in my opinion, was one of the funniest. He wrote, "He said I looked like Boris Karloff."

George Jessel, who is more in demand as a toastmaster than anyone else in show business, principally because he is never at a loss for an apt remark, was evidently speechless when he saw what Gard had done. He signed his without comment. So did Miriam Hopkins, Kent Smith, Juanita Hall, Barbara Stanwyck, Victor Jory, and Yul Brynner. Gilda Gray was the only one who seemed grateful for what Gard had done to her features. She wrote, "At last someone really saw me as I am." Many comics wrote their trade-mark lines on the drawings. Bob Hope wrote "Thanks for the memory," and Bert Lahr put down his traditional "Some fun, eh kid!" Al Hirschfeld, the theatrical caricaturist of the New York *Times,* was drawn for us by one of Gard's successors. "Now I know how it feels," he wrote.

Sometimes, when I look over the walls, I get a little sad. There are so many people who, after making a hit in show business, fell by the wayside, were forced out, or retired. There are scores of them on the list who were big stars at one time; Helen Kane, Gertrude Purcell, Patricia Bryan, Dorothy Mackaill, Bobbie Perkins, Mary Duncan, Janet Gaynor, Louise Fazenda, Helen Chandler, Nell Kelly, Bessie Love. Their pictures are still there in the place.

All told, Gard drew nearly seven hundred caricatures. All during his years with us, he kept two empty spaces near the front of the place. They were reserved, he always said, for my wife and me, but he never seemed in a hurry to do us (perhaps he was afraid my wife would be so angry she would break the contract). Finally I told him I was going to put a caricature of Lee Shubert in one of the spaces. "No, indeed," he said, and that day he drew us. I thought he was gentler with us than with most of his people, and I thought that this proved, after all, that he was a sentimentalist beneath that gruff Russian exterior. Gard died shortly after he drew my wife and me. The date was June 1, 1948, and the cause was a heart attack. No one had ever imagined that anything might have been wrong with his heart; after all, he had served in the navy, and he was always so cheerful that he seemed in excellent health.

One night he gave us a party in his apartment, our whole family—my wife and I, our daughter and her husband, our son and his wife. The next day he headed downtown to see an old friend who'd escaped from Russia. He collapsed in the subway at 42nd Street and Seventh Avenue, and died in the ambulance on the way to the hospital. Among his effects they found five unfinished caricatures which he'd never got around to coloring, and we hung those on the walls. It was more than a year before we replaced him—and then we hired John Mackey, who was followed by Don Bevan, one of the authors of the hit play, *Stalag 17*.

Yet, with all due respect to the new caricaturists, I feel that Alex Gard, who helped to make Sardi's come alive as an institution, will never be replaced. He lives in his drawings on the walls. I never knew a finer or more decent gentleman; he was loved by the whole Sardi family.

CHAPTER TWELVE

Born in Sardi's

O NE NIGHT A FEW YEARS after we opened the new place, a man and his wife came in for dinner as they had on several occasions. I never knew their names, but I had a mild personal interest in them. Shortly after they had come in for the first time, I saw that the lady's condition was beginning to be noticeable. On this night, soon after they ordered, the man jumped up from the table and rushed to the telephone. I looked at the wife, and it seemed to me that she was in pain. Oh, oh, I thought, here it comes. We had had all kinds of things happen in the restaurant, but never a birth; I had always thought that it would be a wonderful experience if we had one, and so I had posted a $1,000 bond to be given to anybody whose child was born in Sardi's. So, when the lady looked as though she might be getting ready to claim the prize, I went over and asked if there was anything I could do. The man was too excited to answer. He came out of the telephone booth, got his wife, and bundled her into a cab. We heard later, from someone, that the baby was born about two hours after they left. I've always wished I'd found out the name of that couple. Perhaps if they read this they will write and let be know how the baby is.

I remember a few other narrow escapes of that kind, but

[174]

nobody ever went home with the bond as long as I had it posted. The only births in Sardi's in my day occurred when the mongrel that Carlo gave Cino had puppies in the basement of the old place. But a good many births of another kind happened—and are still happening, every day. That is, ideas are born: shows are conceived, casting is completed, people are hired and fired, some shows are even financed. I have always been proud that a great deal of actual theatrical business has been carried on across our luncheon or dinner tables; there is no better place to do it. Some time ago, to make it easier, we had telephone jacks installed behind many of the wall tables. Now customers do not even have to leave their seats to carry on their affairs.

It would be interesting to me to know how many plays were first conceived and even partly written at Sardi tables. Certainly the playwrights were always among our most faithful customers. Among those who were frequently on hand were George S. Kaufman and his perennial partner, Moss Hart; Marc Connelly, Arthur Miller, Clifford Odets, Abe Burrows, Alan Jay Lerner, Oscar Hammerstein and Richard Rodgers, Howard Lindsay and Russel Crouse, Sidney Kingsley, Mary Chase, and— well, I can't begin to remember them all, any more than I can remember the number of times I have seen one or another of them go into a kind of trance, their eyes fixed on some distant point, and then take out a notebook or scrap of paper and jot down a note or two. Every once in a while someone would suggest that a play ought to be written about the place, and I believe that one or two writers had a try at it, but nothing ever came of their efforts. Sardi's was once used in a movie, however; it was *The Velvet Touch,* starring Rosalind Russell and Leo Genn.

Since the playwrights and producers were my friends, it would be natural to assume that I made a small fortune investing in plays on tips given me. The fact is, I never put one cent in a show, although I had many opportunities. I could have been a heavy investor in *Oklahoma!* if I had wanted to, and for a time I was strongly tempted. Lawrence Langner had told me he was certain it was going to be a hit, even though he and the other Theatre Guild people had had a terrible time getting money to put it on. Still, I hesitated. I had heard that the Shuberts were not putting money in it, and I decided to follow their example; after all, they had not become the richest and most powerful people on Broadway by making stupid investments. Well, *Oklahoma!* is still cleaning up for its investors.

One other play gave me cause for regret after it became a hit. The producer Brock Pemberton, a good friend, had a play by a woman who lived in Denver. She was unknown, but Brock believed in her script. He was the only one who did. He had gone to virtually all his friends, and he had sent the script to others. Everybody told him he was a fool to think of trying to get it on. Preston Sturges wrote him from Hollywood, urging him to abandon the project. Jules Brulatour, the husband of Hope Hampton and a man whose name cropped up in many backers' lists, refused to invest. When Brock came to me and asked me if I wanted a piece, as usual I said no. Then he went next door to Mackey's Ticket Agency.

Mackey's is run by my old friend Louis Schonceit, whom Robert Sylvester, the columnist, once nicknamed "The Mayor of 44th Street." Lou, who is married to Renee Carroll, our former hat-check girl, has been stage-struck for years. He has been a ticket broker for about thirty-seven years and has made money at it, but he has made more money in investments in various plays. On two or three occasions he has even been a producer. It's safe to say that there's nobody in the Broadway area more respected and loved than Lou, whose agency is the one where most theater people go to buy their tickets. He is a pleasant, bald fellow who wears a hearing aid, and his sense of humor is always in evidence. On the board in his office where he lists the current plays, he lists his friends in the cast as stars. Thus, when Ezio Pinza and Mary

Martin opened in *South Pacific,* Lou omitted their names and put up that of his pal Myron McCormick, who had a minor role. Likewise, when *Guys and Dolls* opened, Lou listed his crony Sam Levene, rather than Robert Alda and Vivian Blaine, who were given star billing by the producers, Cy Feuer and Ernest Martin. Occasionally Lou puts up the name of the press agent for the show, or sometimes the stage manager. If a girl is married but has adopted a stage name, Lou does not recognize it; he puts her up under her husband's name. Thus, Maureen Stapleton, who was in *The Rose Tattoo,* became Maureen Allentuck; and Julie Harris, when she was appearing in *I Am a Camera,* the John van Druten play, was listed on Lou's board as Julie Julien.

Lou's sense of humor held true when Brock Pemberton took him the play that everyone had refused to touch. "I've just about given up," Pemberton said. "I've been working for months, and I haven't been able to get the money together."

"Let me read it," said Lou.

He took the play home that night and began it with some misgivings. They were quickly put aside as he got further into it. By the time he'd finished, he was so excited he wanted to call up Pemberton immediately. It was too late for that, so he did the next best thing. He went to his desk and wrote a check for $10,000. The next day he sent it to Pemberton with a note that said, simply, "Go ahead." It was this check that encouraged Pemberton to go after other backers. Presently he had enough money to bring the play to Broadway. It starred Frank Fay and Josephine Hull in the original cast, and Joe E. Brown and James Stewart played it later in New York and on the road. A successful movie starring Stewart was made from it. It ran for years and is still being played all over the globe. Its name was *Harvey.* Since then its author, Mary Chase, has had two other successes, *Mrs. Mc-Thing* and *Bernardine,* both of which were running at the same time last year.

A producer who was just as good a friend of mine as Pemberton, but not as successful, was Will Morrissey. He first began coming to the old place with Graham McNamee, the radio announcer who gained fame on the old Ed Wynn radio show, and Nils T. Granlund (N.T.G.), who was known for his spectacular girlie shows in the cabarets and theater restaurants. Morrissey was a typical Irishman, of medium height with bushy eyebrows. A fabulously energetic fellow, he was—and is, I suppose—one of the best promoters who ever lived. They called him a "cuff producer," because he could finance and produce shows almost entirely on credit. Frequently he went into production without having a line of the show set down on paper. He would bring in his prospect, usually a wealthy oil man or a rancher, sit him down at a prominent table, and order food lavishly. His air of authority must have convinced the prospect that he was on the level. Will would hum snatches of songs for the proposed show, tell jokes, and do everything but imitate the chorus line. Many times he would wind up with a check or the promise of one. He literally got his backers drunk on words. One time he was caught, but only for a moment. He was producing a show called *Saluta,* starring Milton Berle. One of his prospects expressed interest after he had outlined the show, and said, "Send me a script." Morrissey had not yet had time to get anything on paper, but, operating on the theory that backers almost never read scripts, he grabbed the first one he found in the office and sent that along. I have been told that it was *Strange Interlude,* by Eugene O'Neill. Just before the opening, the backer went to a rehearsal. He was somewhat surprised to find girls, bright costumes, and a comic on the stage.

"This isn't the script you sent me!" he protested to Will.

Nothing could ruffle the Irishman. "Well, well," he said, soothingly, "you know how they're always changing things in rehearsals!"

Once Will told me a fantastic story about a revue he pro-

duced for a cabaret on Columbus Circle. It was during Prohibition. He got the material for the show, the girls, and the
costumes lined up in short order, but he had to bluff his
way on payments until the manager gave him the first week's
check. When the revue opened it was a hit, but somehow
nobody had made things right with the enforcement officers.
After the first night, Will was told to take his show out because the place was due to be padlocked. That didn't stop
him. He went to work on the chief officer, told him how
everybody had to be paid off, told him how he would be
ruined if the show didn't run, and in general sang a very
sad song. It worked; the padlocking was delayed for three
weeks, and in that time he not only paid off everybody, but
also made a small profit.

There is one thing I would like to mention about Will.
Although he often kept me up until four and four-thirty
A.M. while he entertained a prospect, and although he always ordered lavishly, he never owed me a cent. As far as
his business with me was concerned, he was letter-perfect.

Since, as I have stated previously, Ward Morehouse was
always one of our most faithful patrons, it was only right
that something good should happen to him in Sardi's. This
occurred in the new place. One day soon after we opened,
he and Leonard Gallagher, then general manager for Guthrie McClintic, were having lunch at Morehouse's regular
table in the front section. Gallagher suggested that Morehouse, who was such an authority on the stage, ought to
write a play himself.

"By coincidence, I've got one under way," Morehouse
said. "As a matter of fact, the first act is almost finished."

A day or two later he sent the play to Gallagher, who
showed it to McClintic. Both agreed that they should option
it for future production, and they gave Ward a $500 pay-
ment. But eventually, because of casting difficulties, they
had to drop their option. Again Ward came to lunch in
Sardi's, this time with Tommy Jackson, who was playing in

Broadway, the hit by George Abbott and Phil Dunning, presented by Jed Harris. (The girls in *Broadway,* by the way, were good friends of ours; they used to come in after every performance, and so did Lee Tracy, Sylvia Field, Robert Gleckler, and others in the cast.) Jackson became interested in the Morehouse play, and he picked up the option McClintic had dropped. He later got George Abbott to direct it, and it was produced at the Henry Miller Theatre in 1928. It was called *Gentlemen of the Press,* and John Cromwell was in it. Later it was made into a movie by Paramount, starring Walter Huston and Kay Francis. It was one of the earliest talkies.

Ward has another story about a career he helped launch in Sardi's, but he does not like to tell the name of the girl involved. Today she is a big star, but in the late twenties she was so broke she had to borrow a large sum of money. Naturally, no bank was willing to lend money to an actress unless she could produce cosigners. She appealed to Ward, and one day at lunch he and Bennett Cerf, the publisher, signed the note. She later paid the loan back—and it was that money which enabled her to go on living in New York and, eventually, to wind up with the parts that made her famous.

I suppose if all the financial deals that were made in our place could be totted up, they would amount to more than a million dollars. Some of them I knew about as they were happening, but I have long since forgotten the details. The ones I remember best were those involving some of our favorite customers. Not long ago William Liebling, the agent, told of one of the toughest selling jobs he ever accomplished in Sardi's. Liebling is a tiny, gnomelike man who always wears a stiff high collar, odd coat and trousers. He speaks rapidly, with complete sincerity—a quality that sets him apart from a good many ten-percenters. He is the man who sold *Room Service* to RKO Pictures for $255,000, a record price at the time. He got Garson Kanin, the director and playwright, his first job in Hollywood; he put David Wayne into *Finian's Rainbow,* and he practically cast the original company of *A Streetcar Named Desire,* for he sold Marlon Brando, Kim Hunter, Jessica Tandy, and Karl Malden into their parts. The play was written, as everybody must know, by Tennessee Williams, a discovery of Audrey Wood, who is Mrs. Liebling in private life. Mrs. Liebling is rather fabulous herself. Not only did she keep Tennessee Williams alive, working, and encouraged when he was in his formative years, but she also discovered and did the same thing for William Inge, the author of *Come Back, Little Sheba,* and *Picnic.* She was the lady who was most instrumental in getting Carson McCullers to dramatize her novel, *The Member of the Wedding,* which became a hit with Julie Harris, Ethel Waters, and Brandon De Wilde in the cast. It was she, too, who got Maurice Valency, a professor at Columbia University, to do an adaptation of *The Madwoman of Chaillot,* which also was a smash. But to return to her husband's selling job:

Liebling had done considerable casting work for Sam H. Harris. In 1935 he had aided in the casting of *First Lady,* by Katharine Dayton and George S. Kaufman, which was produced at the Music Box with Jane Cowl as the star. The following year, when time came for the show to go on the road, Liebling wanted to put a client of his, the late Ann Mason, in the company. Kaufman advised him not to interfere, since it is generally the right of the star to decide what players will travel with her in the road company. Liebling was determined to get the part for Miss Mason. He approached Miss Cowl and told her about his client, and the star agreed to interview her. At the interview, things seemed to go satisfactorily. A day or two later Miss Cowl changed her mind. Liebling says he suspected that it was because Miss Mason was too attractive, but of course he did not venture that opinion. Nothing he said could cause Miss Cowl to revert to her original decision. He tried to persuade her the next day, and the next. Finally, with the deadline for the road company casting drawing near, he invited Miss Cowl to have supper with him at our place after the evening's performance. It was here that his early training as a singer and minstrel man—he had been on the stage practically from boyhood—came into play. Miss Cowl wanted to take a cab from the Music Box, which was located one block away from our place, in 45th Street. In the cab Liebling began singing some romantic songs from his old days in the vaudeville theaters. In our place he began paying Miss Cowl extravagant tributes on past performances he had seen. He remarked that she had always been one of his favorite actresses. He mentioned that it was a wonderful thing for him to think that not only had her performance in *First Lady* provided continuous work for a cast of about thirty people, but that it had also kept the ushers, stagehands, electricians, and box-office personnel eating happily and supporting their families for nearly a year. He kept talking until most of the other customers had departed. The clock crept nearer two, and passed it. Still he went on talking. Finally, during a lull in Liebling's conversation, Miss Cowl said, abstractedly, as though it were the last thing on her mind, "You know, Mr. Liebling, I think maybe Ann Mason might do for that part after all." Liebling nearly fainted; he was utterly exhausted.

There was one other instance in which an actor practically cast himself into a part in our place—but without doing as much talking as Liebling did. It happened to be our old friend Louis Calhern, who always spends a great deal of time in the place when he is back from his frequent trips to Hollywood. One night when he was sitting in the place after dinner, he got to talking about the works of Ferenc Molnar, the great Hungarian dramatist. He said that he'd always admired Molnar as much as any other playwright of modern times because Molnar wrote roles that gave actors an opportunity to display their virtuosity. "I've always wanted to do a revival of *The Play's the Thing*," he added.

Leonard Lyons, the columnist, heard of this and decided to do something about it. Molnar was a good friend of Lyons; he had been godfather to one of the latter's sons. The playwright was then living quietly at the Plaza in quarters he had occupied for years, seldom venturing forth except for a brief stroll around the Plaza fountain. At night he took his dinner at a tiny restaurant on 58th Street, Macario's. He almost never appeared in any of the restaurants frequented by celebrities. The evening after he had talked to Calhern, Lyons persuaded Molnar to come to Sardi's. He introduced them and they immediately began discussing a revival of *The Play's the Thing.* Then they took the project to Gilbert Miller, who owned the American rights to the play. He, too, was enthusiastic and the production shortly thereafter went into rehearsal. It was an immediate hit, ran nearly a year, and was the play that introduced Faye Emerson to Broadway. Arthur Margetson, who scored a great personal triumph the following season in Ben Levy's *Clutterbuck,* was also in the cast.

Lyons played a part in the birth of another project that was less successful. Shelley Winters, the film star, had met and married Vittorio Gassman, an actor and director, in Italy. When they returned to this country, they decided they wanted to appear together in a play on Broadway. They mentioned this to Lyons in Sardi's. Later that evening Lyons introduced them to Jule Styne, the composer, who also produces shows when he finds a script to his liking (he presented the successful revival of *Pal Joey*). Styne, hearing of Mr. and Mrs. Gassman's interest in a Broadway production, remarked that he had heard of a script about an American actress who became involved with an Italian director in Rome.

"In the Hotel Excelsior?" Miss Winters asked, excitedly.

"I think so," said Styne.

"The suite with the balcony?" Gassman asked, in even greater excitement.

"We can write it that way," Styne said.

From then on the conversation became even more animated, and the very next day Styne took an option on the play. Plans were formulated, but then Miss Winters spoiled them by going into another production. That is, she retired to have a baby. Styne nevertheless produced the show near the beginning of the 1952–53 season. It was called *In Any Language,* and starred Uta Hagen, but although the notices were excellent for her performance, the production did not last very long.

Lyons was also the man, I believe, who first introduced Tallulah Bankhead to Elia Kazan, the director. Lyons says that Miss Bankhead, upon seeing Kazan for the first time, turned to her husband, John Emery, and asked if Turkey was on our side; she thought that the dark-complexioned Kazan was a Turk, and she was so patriotic she wished to have nothing to do with anyone who came from an enemy country. Later Kazan staged *The Skin of Our Teeth,* the Thornton Wilder play in which Miss Bankhead starred. There were rumors at the time that the two of them fought violently all during the rehearsals, but in her autobiography, published last year, she says that they are now good friends.

I have heard that one very successful television program originated one night when a couple of our regular customers were dining with us. The man responsible was Irving Mansfield, the CBS producer who conceived Arthur Godfrey's "Talent Scouts" and "The Stork Club Show," and who also was the first to recognize Sam Levenson, the folk humorist, as a television attraction. Mansfield was having dinner with his wife, Jacqueline Susann, a versatile lady who is actress, playwright, and currently a television star. They remarked to each other that no other place in the city was so popular with actors, and Miss Susann, who used to come in Sardi's in her struggling days in hopes that producers would see her, said that she always felt sad when she saw the actors hanging around, looking hungry for work. "Most of those people are talented," she said, "and in many cases, it's just one small thing that keeps them from being recognized and going on to develop into really successful personalities." Warming up, she added, "There ought to be some sort of— uh—well, *clinic* where actors could go and discuss their problems with experts." Mansfield pointed out that there already were such places—The Actors' Studio, for example, where Elia Kazan, Daniel Mann, and other directors worked with young actors, and also Erwin Piscator's theatrical wing of the New School for Social Research. But already his mind was working. "What's the matter?" his wife asked (Irving is one of the worst hypochondriacs in show business, and she thought he was sick). "Might make one hell of a TV show," he said. "You'd get the actors up there, and they'd have problems, and you'd have this panel, see, and they'd listen, and advise, and maybe make some jokes, and . . ." And he went on like that at length, formulating the program. The next day he broached the idea to some CBS officials. Only one was interested—Hubbell Robinson, Jr. (who, by the way, is the husband of our old friend Vivienne Segal). After many weeks Robinson and Mansfield convinced network officials that the show ought to be given a try. It went on as a simultaneous broadcast and telecast and was an immediate hit.

If there was ever a person who transacted more theatrical business in Sardi's than any other individual, it must have been John Golden, one of my oldest and dearest friends. He needs no introduction to anybody who knows anything at all about the theater; to his credit are such long-running hits as *Lightnin'*, which ran nearly 1,300 performances, *Seventh Heaven, Claudia, Three Wise Fools,* and just last year, the successful revival of *The Male Animal.* Mr. Golden started out on his career, he once told me, as a song writer, and as he grew successful he collaborated with Irving Berlin, Jerome Kern, and Victor Herbert. He was a lyricist. In 1916, having earned around $4,000 in royalties from a song called "Good-bye, Girls, I'm Through," he quit Tin Pan Alley to become a producer—except that he does not say "John Golden Presents," as most producers use the word. He modestly puts on his signs, "John Golden Offers." Once he recruited an actor from Sardi's: the same mongrel dog that Carlo gave to little Cino. It had a walk-on part in his production of *Pigs,* which featured Wally Ford and ran at the Little Theatre. It has been our pleasure to have him as our guest for lunch nearly every day for almost as many years as I can remember. Last year, on June 26, to be exact, there was a party in Sardi's in celebration of his seventy-eighth birthday. It was sponsored by Elliott Nugent, Martha Scott, and Robert Preston, the three principals in *The Male Animal.* Nugent acted as master of ceremonies, and the guests included Mrs. Eleanor Roosevelt, George Abbott, Gertrude Lawrence, Bert Lytell, Chester Morris, Helen Menken, Frances Starr, Paula Stone, Louis Lotito, Jules Munshin, Donald Cook, Ralph Morgan, Francine Larrimore, Peggy Wood, Matt Briggs, and several others. George Abbott recalled that he had worked for Mr. Golden for $15 a week, and Louis Lotito, who now heads the City Playhouse Corporation, remembered that as a boy he had sold songs for Mr. Golden at the old Hippodrome. It was a wonderful party, and nothing could have pleased me more than knowing we were able to make our old friend's birthday a happy one.

Mr. Golden was partially responsible, during a conversation in our place, for the establishment of the famous Antoinette Perry awards—the "Tonys," which are to the theater world somewhat as the Oscars are to moving pictures. But before I tell that story, I must tell about the American Theatre Wing, one of the foremost spontaneous gestures of good will and international friendship ever to come out of this country. Shortly after Germany invaded the Low Countries in World War II, a group of theatrical ladies met in the apartment of Antoinette Perry to discuss what they could do to aid the beleaguered nations. Among the group were Rachel Crothers, the playwright, whose successes included

When Ladies Meet, As Husbands Go, and many others; Vera Allen, the actress, whose appearances included a stint with Katharine Hepburn in *Philadelphia Story* and with Elizabeth Bergner in *The Two Mrs. Carrolls;* Gertrude Lawrence, and Mrs. Louise Beck. The group in a way was an offshoot of Actors' Equity, and at first the women decided to devote their spare time to sewing and knitting for bombed-out civilians. In the beginning they were affiliated with Allied War Relief; after the fall of France, with British War Relief. The officers were Rachel Crothers, president; Antoinette Perry, secretary and chairman of the board; Gertrude Lawrence, Helen Hayes, and Vera Allen, vice-presidents; Mrs. Martin Beck, treasurer; and Josephine Hull, the grand lady known for her performance in *Arsenic and Old Lace, You Can't Take It with You, Harvey,* and so many other plays, as honorary treasurer. The biggest project of this group was the celebrated Stage Door Canteen, which was opened in March, 1942, in the basement of the 44th Street Theatre, practically next door to our place, formerly the site of the old Little Club. The Stage Door Canteen remained open until October, 1945, and I am certain that no other servicemen's canteen in the country was ever as popular. During the first week, more than eight thousand servicemen and women came; nearly five million came in during its three-year existence. The Canteen offered entertainment, food, and nonalcoholic drinks; but perhaps more important to the boys and girls, it offered a chance to dance with lovely actresses and actors, and to be served by such luminaries as Shirley Booth, Alfred Lunt and Lynn Fontanne, Boris Karloff, Vicki Cummings, Marlene Dietrich, and—well, if I go on with this list, I will fill up the book.

The name of Alfred Lunt reminds me of a story about him and Cino. Lunt, in addition to being an actor of the first rank, is also a chef who is as expert as any I know. In the summers, when he and Miss Fontanne are at their place at Genessee Depot, Wisconsin, he devotes himself to cooking.

Whenever he came into our place, I was always as careful as could be of the food we gave him. I often asked his advice about certain dishes. Soon after I retired and Cino took over, I said to him, "You must always be sure that Mr. Lunt's food is faultless." Cino, naturally, was very eager to show the actor that he was a good proprietor. Well, toward the end of World War II, they called me up from the Stage Door. Miss Fontanne was on the telephone, asking for help. "Alfred is in charge of the dishwashers," she said, "and he's getting all confused and mixed up." Cino happened to be home at the time, so I sent him over. Mr. Lunt was up to his neck in soapy water, piles and piles of dishes, and people who were trying to be helpful. "Get me out of this," he begged. Cino's training in kitchens went right into action. He had the stacks of plates put on separate tables, fixed up an extra tub for washing, and got the other volunteers into an assembly line. Mr. Lunt said to him, "Young Sardi, you serve fine food at your place, and you know how to get people seated gracefully—but after this, I know you know how to run a restaurant!"

Lunt was not the only well-known actor who washed dishes. *Everybody* did—and everybody did all the other jobs, too, without complaining. Everything in the Stage Door was donated by people of the theater or by restaurants catering to theatrical customers. Lee Shubert gave the quarters, and the unions of stagehands, electricians, painters, carpenters, and designers decorated them. Acts from night clubs dropped in every evening. On more than one occasion the entire cast of some hit show appeared and went into a repeat performance. Some entertainers would do their specialties, go to the serving tables and work for a while, then come back and do their acts over again. There was something always going on. Many times, when the volunteers were in a jam and help seemed to be short, my wife and I would set some of our kitchen help to making sandwiches, desserts, or roasting meat to take over to the Canteen. It was truly a cooperative enterprise, and one of the most inspiring things I have ever seen. It made you feel good just to be part of it. But don't let me intimate that ours was the only restaurant that helped; there were many, many others, ranging from the Horn and Hardart cafeterias on up to the most exclusive places in town. Jane Cowl and Selena Royle, who appeared in many plays, among them *When Ladies Meet* and *Days Without End,* were cochairmen of the committee in charge of the Canteen. Kermit Bloomgarden, the producer, was business manager. Radie Harris had the job of lining up entertainment.

The Canteen was finally closed because the building had to be vacated and no other building could be found to accommodate it. The Theatre Wing, however, went on, and is still active. Our dear friend Antoinette Perry passed on in 1946. She had had an active life in the theater; she had started out as a child with David Warfield and had played in countless productions, among them the famous ill-fated *The Ladder,* the show that a Texas millionaire kept running so long that at one time people were paid to go and see it. Tony, as we called her, was best known as a director. She was associated with Brock Pemberton, and among her most famous hits were *Strictly Dishonorable* and *Personal Appearance* and *Harvey.* When she died in 1946, all Broadway went into mourning. Shortly after her death Jacob Wilk, a movie company executive, suggested to John Golden at lunch in our place that something really should be done to perpetuate Tony's memory. Mr. Golden, in turn, relayed the suggestion to the Theatre Wing. The members of the board appointed Brock Pemberton as permanent chairman of a committee to select a series of annual awards which would be chosen by secret ballot among the directors. These awards were not necessarily to be "firsts," or "bests," but to be recognitions of commendable contributions to the theater in its various phases.

Today the awards are given each year at a dinner held around Easter time. The public is invited to this dinner.

The Tonys are the only awards given by the professional theater to its own people.

The first Tonys were given in 1947. They went to Patricia Neal for her performance in Lillian Hellman's *Another Part of the Forest;* Helen Hayes, for *Happy Birthday;* David Ffolkes, for his costume sketches for *King Henry VIII;* Agnes De Mille, for her *Brigadoon* dance work; Burns Mantle, for his yearly collection of *The Best Plays* (now being carried on by John Chapman and Garrison Sherwood since Mr. Mantle's death); Ingrid Bergman, for her performance in *Joan of Lorraine;* Michael Kidd, for his *Finian's Rainbow* choreography; Elia Kazan for staging *All My Sons;* Frederic March, for his performance in *Years Ago;* Lucinda Ballard, for her costume designs; Dora Chamberlain, for her courtesy in serving box-office patrons; José Ferrer, for his *Cyrano;* Arthur Miller, for being the best new playwright (*All My Sons*); Jules J. Leventhal, for his prolific backing and producing; and Kurt Weill, for his musical score for *Street Scene.*

There was one other award. I was in California at the time I heard of it. It was my first real vacation in twenty years, just after my retirement, and my wife and I were having a great time visiting old customers who had moved to Hollywood. One day a telegram came, saying that I had been chosen to receive one of the first Tonys. "Vacation or no vacation," I said to my Eugenia, "I am not going to miss that dinner." So we packed up right away and flew back.

They gave me the award at the dinner at the Waldorf. I cannot describe how it made me feel; all I could do was say thank you and sit down. The award was a gold money clip. On it was an inscription that always makes me feel proud when I read it; it makes me feel that I have indeed been a part of the theater. It said, "To Vincent Sardi, for providing a transient home and comfort for theatre folks at Sardi's for twenty years."

I had never used a money clip before, but I have never been without this one.

CHAPTER THIRTEEN

"Luncheon at Sardi's"

T WO OR THREE YEARS AGO our son and his wife, the former
Adelle Rasey, took Jenny and me on a six-week automo-
bile trip from coast to coast. It was a beautiful trip, the best
way to see this wonderful country of ours and the best way
to find out how many nice people inhabit it. All the time
we were gone, all through the twenty-eight states we visited,
we kept in touch with Sardi's every day—not by telephone,
as you might expect, but by means of our radio program.
We heard it all during the trip, and it made us feel close to
home no matter where we were.

"Luncheon at Sardi's" is the name of our program. It is
an interview show, originating right from our restaurant. It
was not the first of its kind; previously, Ilka Chase had had a
similar show emanating from the Waldorf-Astoria Hotel.
But our show has been on the air longer, continuously, than
any other, and today it has many, many imitators. In fact, it
seems to me that almost every time I turn on the radio, I
tune in on a man sitting in a restaurant talking to guest
celebrities.

Our program began around the middle of 1946, and the
people who originated it are still connected with it. First,
there was Gary Stevens, a former press agent turned radio

and television producer ("Twenty Questions" is one of his
shows). There was also Marlo and Minnabess Lewis. Marlo,
then an advertising agency executive, now is producer-direc-
tor of the Ed Sullivan television show on CBS. His wife was
also active in television and radio. Then, too, there was Sid
White, a radio columnist and producer, and Cino and me.
We set up headquarters in our building, upstairs in the
offices of Oscar Kanny Associates. Oscar is another producer
who pitches in to help get top celebrities for our show. He
also produces the "Cracker Barrel Interviews" for Ted Col-
lins on the Kate Smith show on NBC. As soon as we formed
a partnership, we signed a ten-year contract with WOR, of
the Mutual Network, and we were ready to roll.

For a period, "Luncheon at Sardi's" was a network show.
Today it is carried only on WOR, but that station is a
50,000-watter, and as we found out on our trip, the program
can be picked up far away. Igor Gorin, the baritone, who
has been on the show many times, always listens for it when
he is driving around to his concert dates. He has heard it
in the Midwest, he says. When Arthur Mann, of the staff
of the Brooklyn Dodgers, was on the program, his son wrote
him that he heard it on a naval vessel in the middle of the
Pacific. Once we had an important Canadian railroad man on
the show. He was concerned with making arrangements for
the tour of Princess Elizabeth and the Duke of Edinburgh,
and he said, as a joke, that his railroad was going to handle
ninety-five per cent of the trip. "I suppose I can say that
safely, since the program isn't being heard in Canada," he
said. Within a half hour, he received a telegram from the
president of his biggest competing railroad. THANKS FOR GIV-
ING US THAT FIVE PER CENT, it said.

The format of our show is a little different from that of
other talk jockey shows. Most talk jockeys just sit. Ours
moves around from table to table. The northeastern end of
our upstairs dining room is given over to "Luncheon at
Sardi's" each day from twelve-thirty to one-thirty P.M. The

guests sit in tables arranged in a hollow square. There is a large table in the center, where our jockey and his listener-guest of the day sit during the first few minutes. After that, the two of them move from table to table.

The first master of ceremonies on the show was the popular Bill Slater, a tall, genial, gray-haired fellow, one of the most active announcers on the networks. Bill was an ex-West Pointer, and apparently his army training had equipped him to be ready for any emergency. One day all the electric lights went off in the middle of the program. It didn't stop him for a moment; he went right on as though nothing had happened, finishing in darkness with a flashlight in his hand. There was one other time when he worked under a severe handicap. We had had a fire, and had to close for two weeks. During that time we kept the program on the air; but poor Bill had to do his interviews with the carpenters, plasterers and other workmen crashing about in the background! In the fall of 1952 Bill was doing five or six different shows every week. He gave them so much of his time and energy that his doctor finally ordered him to take a rest. He was replaced by his brother Tom, a vice-president in the advertising firm of Ruthrauff and Ryan. It is safe to say that few other people have met as many celebrities in the entertainment business and the sports world as the two Slaters. "Luncheon at Sardi's" features eight guests a day. There are five shows a week, which means forty celebrities a week, or two thousand and eighty a year. The other day we figured that even though many of our guests have repeated, we've presented at least twelve thousand prominent people since we have been on the air.

Since they've met so many, it's only natural that the Slaters, Sid White, Gary Stevens, Irving Cahn, and our show's engineer, Jim Mackenzie-Reid, should have learned a good deal about the nature of celebrities.

They have found, for example, that celebrities almost invariably have professional ball-players as their own personal celebrities. Stars of the theater, Sid White says, invariably become humble in the presence of a Ralph Kiner or a Yogi Berra. Once, when Louis Calhern was on the show, he and Edward Everett Horton refused to pose for a picture unless they could do it with Bob Feller, who was also a guest. Calhern then said he wanted to see Feller pitch that day. "Fine," said Feller. "I'll give you some box seats if you'll get me some tickets to your play!" They arranged the trade then and there. Another time the boys invited in a well-known dance director. He was a very officious man and pretended great impatience with the program. He gave the impression that it was all beneath him. Then he learned that Feller was also scheduled for that day. Instantly he lost his arrogance and pompousness. "Bob Feller!" he cried. "Gee, do you suppose I could meet him?"

Another fact the boys have observed is one I learned early in the business: that the biggest stars are invariably the easiest to handle, the least temperamental, and the most polite. One day they had a small-time comic on the show who behaved like the dance director mentioned above. He tried to impress everybody with his importance. On the same show was a tall, quiet fellow who sat by himself at a corner table. He looked as though he might have been a master in a Midwestern high school, or a young insurance salesman. "Who's that long drink of water over there?" the comic demanded. "Why," said Sid White, "that's Jimmy Stewart." Robert Young showed up one day earlier than his scheduled time. Instead of demanding to be on the show, as a less successful, more self-conscious actor might have done, he apologized profusely and said he hoped the producers wouldn't hold it against him!

It's been the experience of the producers of the show that the biggest names do not always make for the best interviews. Claire Trevor, heroine of countless Hollywood films, developed a bad case of mike fright and was very nervous throughout her interview. "The important thing about any interview," says Tom Slater, "is that the personality, the real personality, of the person gets across to the radio audience."

Guests are invited to the program about two weeks in advance. As long as it's been in existence, only one person has ever crashed the show—and he did it a number of times. He was Irwin Corey, formerly a night-club comic, now an actor on the stage, whose most recent vehicle was *Mrs. McThing,* the Mary Chase comedy which starred Helen Hayes, and in which Brandon De Wilde and Jules Munshin also appeared. Before that, Corey had been in a succession of flops, including *Flahooley,* by E. Y. Harburg; that one starred Ernest Truex, another old Sardi regular. Corey crashed "Luncheon at Sardi's" simply by coming in, sitting down, and jabbering in a kind of French double-talk to the people around him. Bill Slater would take the microphone to his table, sit down, and Corey's language would become even more unintelligible. This used to exasperate and puzzle Sol Zacuto, the waiter who has always been assigned to the show. Zacuto is a member of Sardi's "international family of waiters"—and we have a group that speaks Russian, German, Greek, French, Italian, Spanish, Portuguese, Hindustani, Arabic, and Polish. Sol himself speaks six languages, and he is the show's interpreter. He has translated for Ferrucio Tagliavini, Cesare Siepi, the opera stars, and Helene François, the singer and sister of Denise Darcel. Once Turhan Bey came in, and Sid White told Zacuto to speak to him in his native Turkish. Bey protested, "Hey—haven't you got a waiter who speaks English?" To get back to Irwin Corey, he was the only one who stopped Zacuto. When the comic began his jargon, Zacuto would listen carefully and catch what he thought were a few real words. Then a frown would appear on his face. Finally he would throw his hands in the air and confess that he couldn't understand a thing Corey was saying. It took him a long time to realize that Corey wasn't saying anything.

Corey was not the only eccentric ever to appear, as you

might imagine. One day we had two yogis—or so they called themselves. "How do you like the food?" Bill Slater said to one.

"I'm not so fond of American food," the yogi replied, "but the glassware is very good." And he picked up a tumbler and proceeded to eat it!

His partner was no less strange. When it came her turn, she astonished everybody by getting up, doing a flip, standing on her head, and remaining in that position throughout the interview. Another Hindu guest was the fabulous Kuda Bux, who has been amazing audiences all over the world with his strange powers for more than twenty-five years. Bux is the man who claims to be able to see through solid matter—and for all I know, he can. He allows his eyes to be sealed with dough and his entire head to be bandaged, and then he proceeds to read words written on a blackboard by people he has never met face to face. He did an exhibition of this kind on the show. Sid White asked him if it was true that he once walked on fire, and Bux produced clippings from a British newspaper which recounted a fire-walking demonstration he had made under the auspices of the Royal Society for Psychic Research. "I am working on something new," Bux said to White. "One of these days, I hope to be able to walk on water." We had one other curious guest— Ralph Slater, the hypnotist. This occurred when the show was televised, which happened for a short period two years ago. Slater hypnotized a woman and, to show that she was completely asleep, he held her hand over a flame. These things must be catching. Blanche Yurka, the actress, came to see us and said that she had begun to do yogi exercises. She often stood on her head, she said, and she, too, had an ambition: she wanted to learn to stand balanced on one finger.

Naturally, when guests come to the program, they have to walk through the crowded second floor to get to the corner where Tom Slater sits. A good many stars have used this walk as a sort of popularity gauge, just as the Broadway people test their appeal by walking through the crowded first-floor dining room after the theater. If a sort of whispered ovation goes up, the star can be certain that he is doing well. Oddly enough, however, the boys have found that old-time silent movie stars invariably get the biggest ovation from the diners. We've had many of them on the show—Mary Pickford and Buddy Rogers, Nils Asther, Nancy Carroll, Carmel Myers, Victor Varconi, and Lois Wilson, to mention only a few. There was another huge ovation the day Mrs. Eleanor Roosevelt was on, and still another for Gertrude Berg, the beloved creator of "The Goldbergs." Of all the men who ever appeared, Robert Taylor, just back from Rome, where he had made *Quo Vadis,* drew the biggest chorus of whispers. Ray Milland, Francis Lederer, and William Holden also were given accolades by the assembled customers. The boys declare that Holden can come on the show any time he wants to, for he canceled an important newspaper interview with a syndicated columnist just to appear on "Luncheon at Sardi's."

The guests have given us a number of important "firsts" during the time the program has been on. Mayor Vincent R. Impellitteri, of New York City, first announced his intention of running as an Independent candidate during an interview with Bill Slater. Ours was the first program to present Florence Chadwick after she returned from England, where she had successfully swum across the Channel (we've had, in fact, almost every swimmer of note, including Eleanor Holm, Shirley May France, Johnny Weissmuller, and Buster Crabbe). Any number of people have used their appearances on the show to herald a forthcoming child. Howard Duff, the actor, told for the first time in public that Ida Lupino, his wife, was expecting. Frankie Carle, the orchestra leader, announced proudly that he was about to become a grandfather. Nick Kenny, the radio columnist and song writer, surprised us all by throwing back his head and singing, *a capella,* one of his new compositions. "First time on the air," he said. (Another day, an impromptu jam session began when Gene Krupa, the drummer, picked up knife and fork and began to drum on his plate while Rose Marie, the former child star who scored a big hit with Phil Silvers in *Top Banana,* improvised with snatches of popular songs.) Sid Caesar, who with Imogene Coca is now one of the top television attractions, had been a saxophonist with Shep Fields' band and others before he became a comic. He made one of his earliest radio appearances on our show; and at that time, by the way, he held a reunion with Sid White. Sid, it turned out, had acted as baby sitter for Caesar's parents in the days when the comic was a little boy. The first announcement of *Cinerama,* the new three-dimensional motion picture, was made on our show by Lowell Thomas, Jr., who was associated with his globe-trotting father, the commentator, in backing the enterprise.

Many of our guests let down their hair, either voluntarily or through the charm of Bill and Tom's personalities, and told us some inside stuff that would not ordinarily get into either gossip columns or magazine articles. Paul Lukas let his hair down so far that he didn't even wear it! Appearing at the time with Ethel Merman in *Call Me Madam,* Lukas showed up for the broadcast minus his toupee. Nobody recognized him. (Which reminds me that Lee J. Cobb, one of the finest actors around, whose biggest triumph came a few years ago in Arthur Miller's *Death of a Salesman,* sometimes has lunch downstairs without his hairpiece. Few people recognize him, either.) Mrs. Dorothy Hammerstein, wife of Oscar, gave us a glimpse of the home life of one of our foremost lyric writers. She told us that her husband prefers to work standing up, either at an antique stand-up desk, or strolling about the grounds of his home in Bucks County, Pennsylvania. Nothing disturbs him, Mrs. Hammerstein said, except the vacuum cleaner. When the device is turned on, Hammerstein's inspiration is turned off.

Nancy Olson, the lovely young actress whose first big picture was *Sunset Boulevard,* with Gloria Swanson, told us an amusing story about her husband, Alan Jay Lerner, the lyricist, whose collaborations with Frederick Loewe have produced two hits, *Brigadoon* and *Paint Your Wagon.* Lerner, Nancy said, used to be rather jealous. William Wyler, the director of the picture, had posted a strict rule that no visitors were to be allowed on the set. Lerner had wandered on two or three times anyhow, ignoring the rule. Finally Wyler set up an elaborate practical joke. He instructed William Holden, the romantic lead, to hold a kiss with Nancy as long as they could stand it. He staged this scene when Lerner happened to be on. The kiss was one of the longest in history—it lasted for one, two, three and four minutes. By that time young Lerner began to protest. When he understood that it had been a joke, he felt better—and when he found that Wyler had also brought Brenda Marshall, Holden's wife, on the set, he appreciated it even more. But, Nancy said, that was the last time he came over to watch.

John Loder, the actor, made a confession on our show. He announced that he had once stolen a pipe from Louis B. Mayer. He had been at Mayer's house at a party one afternoon, and happened to see the movie executive's pipe collection. One in particular fascinated him. "If you like it so much, keep it," Mrs. Mayer told him. Loder did; but for months, Mayer kept looking for the pipe, and Loder told us that he'd always felt a little guilty about it.

Marie Powers, who won acclaim as star of Gian-Carlo Menotti's intimate opera, *The Medium,* came on and told of her secret vice. She said that every day she got up between eight and nine—not to practice the scales, as we expected, but to go roller-skating at a Broadway rink. Charles Coburn, one of the most beloved of all our actors, revealed why he wears a monocle. He does not do it because he's English, as many people believe, nor does he do it to look more distinguished. The simple fact, Coburn explained, is that he has astigmatism in one eye, and he feels that eyeglasses are a damned nuisance. When Richard Rodgers was on, he revealed that he and Oscar Hammerstein were worried about the reception of their *Allegro*. After the tremendous success of *Oklahoma* and *Carousel*, everybody was looking for *Allegro*, the first original they had done together, to be a smash hit. Reports had gone out, Rodgers said, that it was sold out months in advance. Both he and Oscar were worried because such reports often drove people away from the box office—nobody who wants to see a show wants to wait months to get in. As it turned out, the show was not oversold; it was the team's only failure.

Soon after Renzo Cesana, "The Continental," became a television sensation by winking intimately at his female audience, offering them champagne and soft words, and generally behaving like a lounge lizard, we invited him on the show. After a few preliminary questions, he was asked what kind of champagne it was in the glasses he held out to his unseen lady friends. Cesana's face fell. "It isn't champagne," he said. "It's ginger ale."

Tony Curtis, one of the fast-rising younger movie stars, came to "Luncheon at Sardi's" and told us several things we had not known before. The most astonishing was that just a few years ago he had been a shoeshine boy, and that one of his favorite stands had been outside Sardi's. During the years I got to know most of the familiar faces along 44th Street, but I must admit I do not remember him. "I used to shine shoes outside the place and watch the stars go in," Tony said. "I never thought I would get inside for lunch."

The program has helped several people, I am happy to say. Once Imogene Coca, then a night-club entertainer, came on looking very sad. When Bill asked her why she was so mournful, she told him that she had just had several song arrangements made at considerable expense—but she'd lost them. She thought she'd left them in a taxi, she said. The very next day a listener who'd heard her brought them in. Another time Joan Lorring, the actress, said she couldn't find an apartment. We were besieged with telephone calls, and a few days later she had a place of her own. Two of our listener-guests later went on to become celebrities in their own right. One was Jackie Loughery, a beauty contest winner who later got a contract in Hollywood and married Guy Mitchell, the popular singer. Another was Dolly Martin, who had just come to New York, fresh from an Indiana college. She's now an actress, doing very well in television and radio. Gary Stevens tells about another youngster who had asked him time and again to put her on the show. Her name was Susan Cabot, and she was singing in a night club in Greenwich Village. "Sorry," Gary said, "but we can only put celebrities on the show." Well, Susan Cabot left New York, went out, and proceeded to make a name. The next thing Gary knew, she was on the show as a celebrity. "See, I made it all by myself!" she said.

Several times the show has been marked by brilliant interviews or exchanges. But the two most sparkling female guests were not from show business. They were Fleur Fenton Cowles, the lady who helps edit *Look* and other publications owned by Gardner Cowles, her husband; and Sylvia F. Porter, the economics writer on the New York *Post*. They were both so lively that many people dining in Sardi's thought they were actresses. The late Gertrude Lawrence, one of our favorite customers, was always a welcome guest. Few people in my memory possessed such sparkle; her personality fairly brightened the room. She was always a good sport, always ready for a laugh. One day when she was a guest of the show, Jack Leonard, the comic, happened to be on at the same time. Leonard weighs a good three hundred pounds, and his brash, boisterous humor stems from the burlesque circuits and the borsch belt. Throughout the show he kept Miss Lawrence laughing with his wit. She said she had never heard a funnier man. He told her that he was going to see her in *The King and I*, and she told him to be sure to come back and see her in the dressing room afterward. "Me?" said

Leonard. "I'd never be able to get through the door!" As
Miss Lawrence was leaving, she topped all his jokes with a
serious remark, typical of her. "My only hope," she said, "is
that when you see our show, I make you cry as much as I've
laughed today." For once, Leonard was stopped; he could
not think of a line. When he went back to see her after her
performance, his ordinarily cheerful face was grave. He took
off his hat. "Lady," he said, "you did it."

And her spirited exchange involved Claire Luce, the actress who is often confused with Clare Boothe Luce, the author of *The Women,* and wife of Henry R. Luce, the publisher of *Time* and *Life.* Miss Luce—the actress—had as partner Lefty Gomez, the former pitcher for the New York
Yankees. She had heard of Lefty, but as she quickly demon-
strated, she didn't know too much about baseball. She opened
the conversation by asking Lefty what he was doing now
that he was no longer active in big-league ball.

"I'm with a Yankee farm outfit up in New York State,"
Gomez said.

"How long've you been there?" Miss Luce asked.

"Oh, two years."

"How do you like it?"

"Well, it's not bad," Lefty said, "but sometimes I still wish
I was back in action. I may be getting along, but I'm still
active."

"I wouldn't feel too badly," Miss Luce said. "After all, it's
wonderful of the Yankees to have a farm for you old fellows
to retire to!"

Just then it was time for Miss Luce to go on the air; the
perplexed Lefty never did get a chance to explain that a
"farm club" was not exactly an old ball-players' home.

Basil Rathbone managed to let his wit and presence of
mind carry him gracefully through an encounter with an
excited customer the day he was on the show. Rathbone had
arrived clad in a dark blue suit, with a blue shirt and blue
tie, all of which, as he remarked, made him feel like a rolled-

up umbrella. The sight of him was too much for one lady. She rushed up to him and said, "My God, it's Basil Rathbone!" Then, when she realized her mistake, she appeared ready to burst into tears. Rathbone patted her shoulder to reassure her. "Never mind, Madame," he said, "I'm used to it. I've been called everything. I've even been called Basal Metabolism."

The show was not without its share of embarrassing moments. There was the day, sad to relate, when one of the waiters knocked a plateful of food into the lap of Dorothy Claire, the singer who followed Ella Logan into the cast of *Finian's Rainbow*. When Gene Stanlee, "Mr. America," came to visit us, he was not wearing a coat. We have always had a rule barring men without coats, and for an emergency we keep a few spares in the cloakroom. A bus boy was sent downstairs for a coat and told to bring the largest. When Gene put it on, the sleeves were still six inches too short! Once we nearly had a free-for-all. Al Capp, the Li'l Abner cartoonist, came on the show and mentioned that he had once been in the employ of Ham Fisher, the creator of Joe Palooka. Something he said must have irritated Fisher, for he came in the next day and demand to be allowed to give his side of the story. Another battle, this one a more amiable one, occurred when Fred Finkelhoffe visited us. He had been the author, with John Monks, Jr., of the play *Brother Rat*, one of George Abbott's greatest successes. The play was set at Virginia Military Institute, where Finkelhoffe had been a student. Bill Slater, ever the West Point man, jokingly asked Fred if V.M.I. was not called "The West Point of the South." Fred shook his head solemnly. "No," he said, "it's the other way around. We call West Point the V.M.I. of the North!"

It was always a great treat for us to have comics on the show; they never failed to brighten the proceedings. When Milton Berle arrived, he started off by pointing to the other guests and saying, "What are all these people doing here?" He was told that they, too, were guest stars. His face fell.

"But," he said, "the show is only an hour long—how could you *do* that to me?" Jack Carter and Dean Murphy, both excellent impersonators, sat next to each other when they were on the show. Each refused to talk in his own voice; they kept us laughing by answering all questions in the voices of other celebrities. Some of our happiest moments were with Paul Winchell, the ventriloquist. He never spoke for himself; Jerry Mahoney, his dummy, did all the talking. Larry Storch once came to see us and, without warning, began trying out an entirely new routine he had devised that morning. Jimmy Savo, the pantomimist, was very serious and reserved all through his interview, except when he was asked where he came from. He drew himself up and said, "I'm a Bronxtonian." Gary Merrill, the husband of Bette Davis, drew several laughs when he walked in clad in summer knee-length shorts. He was not the only visitor who proved unexpectedly to be a comic. Cab Calloway, the bandleader, had the audience roaring as he went through his own dictionary of bop-musician terms. As he finished, he said to Bill Slater, "Man, you sure do a cool, cool interview!" Jimmy Dorsey, the band-leader, was another witty guest. Reminiscing about his early days, when he and his brother Tommy were just starting out with their own band from their home town in the coal regions of Pennsylvania, Jimmy said that they had several highly unprofitable months. He began telling us of some of the dismal places they played. "Man," he said, "we played Atlantic City once, in a place so big and so empty that when one of the waiters dropped a tray of dishes, three people got up to dance." And of course, we always had many, many laughs when our old friend Sam Levene, one of the most faithful of the Sardi family, came on the show, as he did many times.

There was only one guest who ever gave us real trouble. His name is familiar to almost every American who has ever taken a motor trip: Duncan Hines. He and Bill had a pleasant interview. Hines told of his most recent travels and his latest books. When he finished, he called for his check.

"No check, sir," Sol Zacuto said.

"But I must have a check," Hines said.

"You're our guest, Mr. Hines," Sid White said to him.

"That's very nice of you," Hines said, "but as long as I have been dining around the country, I have always paid my own way."

"But you don't understand," Gary Stevens said. "You came on the program as our guest. You're Sardi's guest for luncheon."

"I always pay my own way," said Hines, firmly. He waved again at the waiter. "Check, please," he said.

Well, they finally talked him out of it—I think. I was not in on the discussion. If I had been, I would have told Mr. Hines what a good time we'd had following his advice on our motor trip—all his recommendations were splendid. But I would not have got into the argument. After all, I am a restaurant man, first and last—and what restaurant man would dare get into an argument with Duncan Hines?

CHAPTER FOURTEEN

Some Sardi Specialties

NOW WE COME TO ONE of the subjects closest to my heart: cooking. I am certainly not claiming any ability as a cook, but as far back as I can remember, I have always been interested in the preparation of fine food. When I worked in restaurants in London, I used to watch the chefs enviously; it seemed to me that they were the aristocracy of the business. Whenever I could get a minute away from the dishwashing sink, I would go over and hang around the stoves, asking questions, observing how the chefs worked. Sometimes I would try to cook something myself, and I was always overjoyed when it turned out to be good.

I think the reason I was so fascinated by the chefs and their work was the simple fact of my having been born in Italy. To my way of thinking, Italians are born cooks. They have had to be—necessity is the mother of invention, they say, and I believe that Italians became the best cooks of all nationalities because they had so few working materials. When you are limited as to ingredients, you fall back upon your ingenuity; you try to see how many different ways you can prepare a certain meat or vegetable. Many people declare that the French are better cooks than Italians, but I have heard that it was the Italians who set the French on the path when Catherine de Medici brought her household cooks to Paris. Later, Napoleon carried Italian-French cooking with him to all parts of Europe during his conquests, and that is how the reputation of the French came to be established. Yet it is a fact today that in most fine French restaurants in this country, the cooks are Italians! But—I do not want to start an argument about which nation produces the best food.

While my wife and I were actively operating Sardi's we had only four different chefs in thirty-odd years. We lost two to Hollywood; one went out to work in another restaurant, and another went out to get in the movies. (Indeed, he did get in—as a chef working in the commissary of one of the big studios!) Today, Sardi's has two very reliable men: Secundo, who is first chef, and Primo, who is second chef. We are lucky to have them, for first-class chefs are harder and harder to hire. Secundo and Primo's style of food preparation might be described as Italian-French-American. The kitchen in Sardi's was never planned over a definite system; it simply evolved, over a period of years. As I have said, my wife and I did most of the cooking during the first decade. We put on our menu some dishes we brought from Piemonte, some we had learned in other places, some typical American specialties, and some we invented ourselves. Several dishes which later became Sardi favorites were devised especially to please certain customers. When you take care of the same group of people day in and day out over a period of years, you get to know a good deal about their preferences, and that enables you to plan a menu which will satisfy them.

I have often been asked if I found theatrical people to be more or less finicky about their food. I cannot honestly say that this would be true. One thing I did notice, while Jenny and I were in the restaurant, was that many of our friends had one particular dish which they would order in preference to all others. I remember particularly Melville Cooper, the English actor who is almost always in our place around lunchtime when he is in New York. I believe I could have given him charcoal-broiled lamb chops, peas with a pinch of sugar

and fresh mint, and boiled potato with parsley butter every
day for a year and he would never have tired of it. John
Golden was equally consistent. Whenever he saw a dish of
mussels going by, he would suddenly change his previous
order and demand mussels *marinara*—unless he had first
ordered chicken and oyster pie, another of his long-time
favorites. Jane Cowl always asked me for oysters on the half-
shell, stuffed with red caviar; Beatrice Lillie liked to substitute Beluga caviar for red. Whenever Edmund Gwenn was
playing in the neighborhood, he would have us send his dinner to his dressing room on matinee days—and his choice was
almost invariably broiled lamb kidney with parsley butter
and Canadian bacon. Katharine Cornell and Guthrie McClintic usually started dinner with a coleslaw salad and hot
dressing which we named after Miss Cornell, and then went
on to spaghetti and *marinara* sauce with a little chopped red
pepper added to it. I taught Miss Cornell to make that sauce
years ago, and she still makes it sometimes when she and her
husband have guests at home. Shirley Booth was always par-
tial to another house specialty, our Supreme of Chicken à la
Sardi. The late John Drew was extraordinarily fond of Calf's
Liver Venezziana; Alfred Drake always asked me for Osso
Buco and Risotto Milanaise. The last time I saw Ezio Pinza,
he was eating heartily, but it was not an Italian favorite—it
was corned beef and cabbage! The Shuberts, who came into
our place frequently, were very careful eaters, especially Lee;
he liked fish, especially whitefish, and the second joints of
chicken or turkey. Young John Shubert preferred green
noodles fixed with a special raw green sauce made with fresh
basil leaves. In our family there have been two favorites over
the years, *bagna cauda* and *polenta*. I will put down the
recipe for the former presently; the latter is an Italian corn-
meal mush, eaten with rabbit, squirrel, or other game stews.
Polenta, as I have mentioned elsewhere, was Paul Whiteman's favorite; he liked it with small Egyptian quail. As for
me, there is one dish I have always enjoyed above all others

ever since I have been in this country. It is that old American stand-by, ham and eggs.

If credit for Sardi's cooking can be given to any one person, that would have to be my wife. Many people used to rush right by me and go to where she was sitting to consult with her about their food. I was always pleased when that happened, for she was—and is—a grand cook. Other customers used to ask for John Brasi, our manager, to fix their salad dressings in his own special way. Both Mrs. Eleanor Roosevelt and Max Gordon, the producer, would call for Brasi whenever they came in. Brasi's dressing for Mrs. Roosevelt was a simple one, consisting simply of oil, vinegar, garlic, English mustard, and a drop of Lea and Perrins sauce. The catch is that Brasi would never reveal the exact quantities! For Max Gordon, he would always make a salad of cottage cheese with some chili sauce, French dressing, and chives.

Before I put down some of our favorite Sardi recipes, I want to tell about the first Sardi product ever to be sold in a can. There is a story behind it. During the war, when meat was hard to get, I did not want to go into the black market. Therefore, we began serving as many meat substitute dishes as possible. Among the most popular of these was *Canelloni*, which I called *Canelloni* à la Ripley, because it was the favorite of the Believe-It-or-Not cartoonist. It was always the first thing he would order when he came back to New York and took up his headquarters in our place. Well, people must have liked our *Canelloni* a great deal, because they began calling up from all over the country, asking us to pack it or freeze it and send it out. Our chefs began working on a sauce for the dish which could be transported, and they came up with a good basic white sauce. When Cino came back from the marines, he began experimenting with this sauce. He found that any number of dishes could be made with it. Finally he found a way of canning it, and today it is sold in groceries as Sardi's Jiffy White Sauce. Some of the recipes following call for one can of this sauce, but if you wish you can substitute sixteen ounces of a white sauce of your own make.

So, on to the recipes. These are favorites of Jenny's and mine. Some of them are on the Sardi menu today; some of them were on it at various times in the past:

French-fried Zucchini and Zucchini Antipasto

It was always amazing to me to find that some foods which were familiar to me in my youth were new and strange to people I met in this country. Broccoli, for example. One day, when I served a nice dish of broccoli to a man, he wouldn't eat it because he said it tasted like grass. Another woman I knew, upon being served asparagus for the first time, cut off the tender tips and ate the tough stalks! But of all the vegetables I served, none ever caused the amount of comment that zucchini did. Whenever I had it on the menu, I knew that some customer would question me about it and that I would have a tough time getting him to eat it. One day, for example, a man called me over, pointed to the world "zucchini" on the menu, and asked me what it was. Now, I didn't want to tell him it was Italian squash, because I'd had previous experience with people who said they wouldn't eat squash of any kind. So, I told him, "It's vegetable marrow."

He looked at me and said, "So, zucchini is vegetable marrow, eh? Well, what is vegetable marrow?"

"Well," I said, "it's zucchini."

He still was not convinced that he ought to try it, so I told him I would send him some with the compliments of the house. In the kitchen, I had them cut the zucchini like French-fried potatoes, roll the pieces in flour, and fry them in deep fat—again, just like French-fried potatoes—until they were a golden color. When the waiter served the zucchini hot with the main course the man ordered, he stared at the pieces suspiciously for a moment and then tried one apprehensively. Then he tried another. Well, I tell you, he almost finished that plate of zucchini before he even tasted his meat!

He sent for me and said, "Say, this is very good! What did you say it was called?"

"Italian squash," I said. You should have seen his face!

I had similar experiences with broccoli and zucchini at least a hundred times, but today I am happy to say they are two of the most favorite vegetables served in the restaurant.

Now, here is another good way to prepare zucchini. This is an appetizer, but it can also be eaten as a salad with the main course.

As in the recipe above, you peel and cut zucchini in the same way that you cut potatoes for French-frying. Fry the pieces in oil until they are golden brown. Remove from the fire and place in a deep dish. Now, in a separate saucepan take one cup of olive oil, a chopped garlic clove, some well-chopped sage leaves, pepper and salt to taste, and cook gently for five minutes. Add one cup of vinegar and allow it to mix. Leave it on the fire a minute longer. Pour this hot sauce over the zucchini in the deep dish and make sure it covers each piece. Put the dish in the refrigerator and keep it twenty-four hours or more; serve it cold. You can preserve zucchini this way for as long as ten days. It makes a wonderful antipasto.

Katharine Cornell Salad

This is the salad we had to remove from the menu because so many people, after they had ordered it, found that it contained too much garlic. We named it after Miss Cornell because she was so fond of garlic in large quantities that she often ordered the salad and sometimes even asked that more garlic be added. The garlic may be added to taste.

First shred as much white cabbage as you estimate you will need for the number of people you are serving. Shred it the way you would prepare it for coleslaw. Next, take a can of fillets of anchovies and turn them into a frying pan. Let them simmer over a low heat, meanwhile adding a few ounces of olive oil, about an eighth of a pound of butter, and as much garlic as you wish, sliced very thin or minced well. Allow this mixture to remain on the fire, still over the low heat, until the anchovies are completely dissolved and mixed with the other oils. Now add two tablespoons of strong vinegar or, if you prefer, lemon juice. Meanwhile, in another frying pan, fry as many strips of bacon as you wish. Let the bacon get very crisp, take it off, and dry the grease out of it. It should be crumbly.

Put your shredded cabbage in a deep salad bowl. Pour over the anchovy-garlic-oil mixture. Crumble the bacon in your fingers all over this, and it's ready to serve.

Bagna Cauda

This is one of the things that led to my downfall the time my friends and I were on our way to report for the army. It has always been a favorite dish of mine, and my entire family loves it. But like the Katharine Cornell salad, it may be a bit too much for people who do not like garlic. I remember one day last year my wife and I had some friends over, made *bagna cauda,* and ate it almost to the exclusion of everything else. Well, the next day, when I took the train to Manhattan, I was ashamed to sit next to anybody I knew—and in fact, I was ashamed to sit next to strangers!

To make it, you put about a half cup of olive oil and a couple of teaspoons of butter into either a frying pan or a chafing dish, and heat until the butter melts. Mince six or seven cloves of garlic and put them in, and then turn in a can of fillets of anchovies; salt and pepper to taste. Now keep it heated over a slow fire—or in the chafing dish. Take a piece of bread in one hand and some cardo, or green pepper, or celery, in the other. Dip the vegetable into the hot mixture, take a bite of it and a bite of bread—and be prepared to dodge your neighbors! Some people—myself included—have been known to make an entire meal of it.

Pasta Sauces

There are so many ways of preparing *pasta* that I almost hesitate to recommend any specific one. All I can say about the spaghetti or macaroni itself is that you ought to get a good reliable brand, and do it according to the directions and to your own preference—either soft, or *al dente,* or hard enough to be thoroughly chewed. As a rule, eight ounces of *pasta* should be cooked about ten minutes in angrily boiling water to which one tablespoon of salt has been added. The best spaghetti in the old days came from Naples, but today, because of improved methods of manufacture, the American brands are better than any made in Italy. The last time I was over there, I could hardly bear to eat the *pasta.*

There are certainly as many sauces as there are ways to cook *pasta* itself. As for me, I like it best simply with butter and grated cheese, preferably Parmesan. It tastes better, by the way, if the butter is put into the spaghetti in a lump, and melted by working the pasta around in the pan—*not* by melting the butter and pouring it over.

For many years my family and I have been spending our summers at Southold, in Suffolk County on Long Island, one of the most beautiful spots on the entire island. Out there my son-in-law, Frank Gina, sometimes goes crabbing. He makes a splendid spaghetti sauce when he comes home with his catch, cooking cut-up crabs in a sauce made with olive oil to which has been added garlic, parsley, fresh tomatoes, and *orégano* to the taste of the family. As a matter of fact, any sauce made with fish is good. You can make an excellent one by simmering a can of minced clams in olive oil and adding parsley, chervil, some onion, and whatever other herbs you may enjoy.

The meat sauce I like best is, like most good sauces, very easy to make. First, fry one small chopped onion in about one-quarter cup olive oil until it's light brown. Then add one-half pound chopped meat or sausage meat and let it simmer until the raw color has gone away. Then add one small can of tomatoes, salt and pepper to taste, and allow that to simmer for three quarters of an hour or a full hour if you think it necessary. That's all there is to it.

One of the best sauces I know is a raw green one. You take as many fresh basil leaves and as much garlic as you desire and pound them together with a mortar until liquefied. Add Romano or Provolone cheese, add as much olive oil as you wish, and stir all ingredients together. This is called *al pesto*.

Noodles Al Magro

This dish is especially for fast days. Chop an onion and simmer it until golden brown in olive oil. Add a laurel leaf and a clove of garlic, well chopped. Add one can of tomatoes, reduced and drained, or the equivalent in fresh tomatoes, and allow to cook over a slow fire for about twenty minutes. Turn into this a can of French peas, and allow the mixture to cook another five minutes or so. Now add a can of tuna-fish in oil, wait until the fish is heated, and serve over either white or green noodles. It should be explained here that all quantities are approximate in these recipes. I have reduced them from those used in the restaurant kitchen. If you are an experimental cook, you will not have any trouble adding or subtracting for your home needs. The dish above, with about a half pound of noodles, will serve four nicely.

Veal Agro-dolce

The translation of this dish means "sweet-sour veal." It is very simple and easy to make, and can make you a good supper when you do not have much time to spend in the kitchen. Get some veal steaks or strips about one inch thick, dip them in white flour, and cook on both sides in a skillet until golden brown, adding salt and pepper to taste. Remove the veal, add water to the pan to make a little gravy, and put in one teaspoon of sugar and two of white vinegar. Cook this for about three minutes, pour the mixture over the *scallopine,* and serve. A good companion for this is:

Asparagus Milanaise

Cook a bunch of fresh asparagus in salted water until tender. It usually takes about fifteen minutes. Drain and place about six stalks on each plate. Sprinkle with grated Parmesan cheese, salt and pepper as you wish. While the asparagus is cooking, brown some butter in a skillet. When it is brown and bubbling, pour it over the cheesed asparagus. Some people like a gently fried egg atop this dish.

Canelloni À La Ripley

If there is one dish that tops all others in popularity in our place, it is this one. We have it on the menu every day, and people never seem to get tired of it. It's easy to prepare, too; the hardest thing about it is getting the French pancakes thin and light enough.

If you have a recipe for French pancakes that you use as a matter of course, use it. Otherwise, try this one: heat one cup of milk and two tablespoons of butter in a saucepan. When it is slightly cooled, beat in two already-beaten eggs, a half cup of sifted flour, a teaspoonful of baking powder, and a half teaspoon of salt. This is the batter. The cakes should be very thin. These ingredients make about 20 three-inch-in-diameter cakes.

Now make a stuffing with chopped chicken, a little pork sausage meat, cooked and chopped spinach, all in about equal parts. Add grated cheese, salt and pepper, and a pinch of thyme. Run the stuffing through a grinder a couple of times until it is well ground and mixed.

Cover each pancake with a thin layer of the stuffing and roll it up. Put about three for each person on individual pie plates or baking dishes. Make a sauce to cover the pancakes from one can of Sardi's Jiffy White Sauce to which Parmesan

or some other cheese has been added. Put under the broiler
for about five minutes, or until the sauce is brown and crusty.

Risotto Con Rane

Simmer a chopped onion in butter until golden brown,
then add two cups of rice and a pinch of saffron. Stir and
continue to simmer for about five minutes.

Put a can of chicken or beef consommé in a saucepan on
the burner next to the skillet with the rice. Gradually add
consommé to the rice, stirring continually, keeping the rice
at the boiling point until it is completely cooked.

Meanwhile, prepare some cleaned frogs' legs by dipping
them in flour and sautéing them in butter for about five
minutes. Add the frogs' legs to the rice about five minutes
before you serve them. Top each portion with grated Parmesan cheese.

Kidney Campagnola

Take a dozen lamb kidneys, remove the skin and cut in
quarters. Chop two cloves of garlic and a few sprigs of parsley. Sauté the kidneys for five minutes in olive oil, then add
the parsley and garlic. Cook five minutes longer, then toss in
a dash of red wine as you are about to serve.

Lobster All'Inferno

Cut lobster meat in cubes. Sauté one chopped onion in
olive oil until brown; add two chopped cloves of garlic and
cook for two minutes more. Then add the lobster and a half
teaspoon of red pepper. Cook this five minutes before adding
a can of tomatoes, including the juice. Cook this gently for
about twenty minutes. You can use lobster in the shell for
this dish; if you do, increase the cooking time by ten minutes.

Veal Ucceletti

Get thin slices of young veal, about three to a person.
Spread each with olive oil, add salt and pepper, and lay the

fillets flat on a chopping board. Now make a stuffing of chopped onion, garlic, bay leaf, cooked spinach, and cooked rice, and add some butter, some olive oil, and some chopped mushrooms. Put this through a mincing machine or grinder and cook it for about fifteen minutes in a frying pan. Now spread the stuffing over the veal slices. Roll and tie with thread or string. Place in a pan with a little butter, let the veal get brown and then add one-half cup of consommé or broth. Cook over a slow fire for thirty minutes, and at the end add a dash of sherry wine. Don't forget to remove the thread before serving!

Supreme of Chicken À La Sardi

Another of our specialties in Sardi's. Boil a fresh fowl. When it is tender, remove it and slice off the white and dark meat. Place this in a deep dish with a little of the chicken broth and some sherry. Allow the meat to soak for about ten or fifteen minutes. Now, in individual oven pans or dishes, place a layer of tender asparagus tips (precooked), and a layer of dark meat, another layer of asparagus, and a layer of white meat. If you wish, add a bit of the broth and more sherry. Cover each portion with a Supreme sauce made with one can of Sardi's Jiffy White Sauce to which a bit of the broth has been added. The Supreme sauce should be fairly thick. Sprinkle grated Parmesan cheese on top, and put under the broiler for about five minutes if the chicken is warm or ten if it is cold.

French Style Rabbit

A very simple late-supper snack, as delicious as it is easy to make. Grate one cupful of Swiss Gruyère cheese. Beat one egg for each cup of cheese. Mix together with a wooden spoon, adding a teaspoonful of butter. Pour the mixture into an enameled saucepan or a double boiler; cook it slowly, stirring constantly, until it reaches the thickness you desire.

Serve on toast or in a warm dish with toast on the side. Some people prefer this to a sweet dessert.

Rice and Potato Soup

Very quick and economical. Take one small slice of salt pork—about one eighth of a pound—chop it well, and simmer it in a pot with one small chopped onion until the onion turns golden. Now add about one quart of warm water and two bouillon cubes and bring to a boil. Add three potatoes, well diced, and allow them to boil for five minutes. Now add one cup of rice and allow to boil ten minutes or more—until the rice is cooked to your taste. As this soup is served, it may be sprinkled with Parmesan cheese.

Pickled Butterfish

Get six butterfish, each weighing at least one-quarter pound or a little more. Clean them, dip each in white flour, and gently fry them in olive oil until they are golden brown. Remove from the fire and dry them. Now chop a medium-sized onion and one clove of garlic, and put the two in a frying pan and simmer until golden. Keep adding olive oil until there is nearly a cup in the pan, and then add one-half cup of vinegar and let it all simmer a few minutes. Now put the butterfish in a deep dish and cover it with this hot sauce. Allow it to remain in the refrigerator for about twenty-four hours before serving. Bring to the table cold. This makes a wonderful appetizer, but is also a very good main dish.

Filet of Flounder, Bishop

Get a flounder that weighs about two pounds. If you can filet it, fine; if not, the fish-market man will be glad to do it for you. But have him wrap the bones and head for you to take home, for you will need them. Cook them in water to make a fish broth, strain it, and then add salt, pepper, a slice of lemon, a slice of onion, and the filet of flounder. Cook it in the broth for ten minutes and remove the fish.

Strain the broth again and let it boil until it has reduced by about half. Now add one small glass of dry white wine and let it boil for five minutes more. Put in two tablespoons of butter and stir well. Cut two hard-boiled eggs in quarters and arrange them around the flounder on a plate. Pour on the sauce and a dash of paprika and serve.

Skate

When we are fishing at Southold, we sometimes hook a skate. Many people throw this fish away, believing it no good to eat, but if done properly it's delicious. Only the wings are good to eat, however. Boil them in water with salt, pepper, a slice of lemon, and a slice of onion for about ten minutes. Remove the fish, let it drain and remove the skin; it comes off easily when it is scraped with a fork. Put the skate on a platter and sprinkle it with chopped parsley and a few capers. Melt about three tablespoons of butter in a pan, let it cook until it is almost burnt, and then add two tablespoons of vinegar. Pour this over the skate and serve.

Chicken Livers Madeira

Melt about two tablespoons of butter in a frying pan, and add a pound of chicken livers and two fresh mushrooms, sliced. Sauté the livers and mushroom slices for a few minutes, then add salt and pepper and three tablespoons of olive oil and cook for five minutes more. Pour over a half glass of sherry or Madeira wine and serve. A little wild rice goes well with this.

Chicken and Oyster Pot Pie

This is the one dish that will make my friend John Golden turn down his favorite mussels. Use about one cup of white meat of chicken, diced, and six oysters per person. Put the chicken at the bottom of a pie dish, and sprinkle it with salt, pepper, and a pinch of nutmeg. Cover with a layer of chopped mushrooms. Now put in the oysters, a few more mushrooms, more salt and pepper and a little nutmeg. Garnish with parsley. Cover the whole with a sauce made with a can of Sardi's Jiffy White Sauce to which about one cup of oyster liquor has been added. Cover the dish with a pie crust, poke it, put in the oven and bake for about fifteen minutes.

Zabaione

This is one of my favorite desserts, and very much in demand in the restaurant. It requires constant attention. Take four yolks of eggs, eight tablespoons of sweet sherry or Marsala wine, and four tablespoonfuls of granulated sugar. Combine them and beat or whisk them until the sugar is dissolved. Now cook the mixture over a very low flame or in a double boiler, beating it continually until it achieves the thickness of a heavy cream. Never allow it to boil! Serve it in a cup or glass with a few ladyfingers on the side.

Dessert Strawberries

One of the simplest and yet most elegant of all our desserts. Wash, pluck, and dry one quart of fresh strawberries. Put them in a dish and sprinkle over them about three tablespoons of granulated sugar. Now pour over one pint of sparkling red wine, although still wine will do, too. Place in the refrigerator an hour or more before serving. A little grated lemon or orange peel goes well atop the berries.

Special Recipes for Use with Sardi's
Jiffy White Sauce

The following recipes are only a few of many that can be made with the Sardi's Jiffy White Sauce. (Your own white sauce may be substituted.)

Clam Bisque

There are two ways to make this delicious soup:

1. Put six ounces of chopped clams (use canned clams if you wish) in a saucepan with two cups of water. Let it boil

two minutes. In a separate saucepan, put one can of white sauce and one cup of milk and bring to the boiling point. Smooth this mixture with an egg beater or whisk. Combine with the clams. Season with one teaspoon of salt and a quarter of a teaspoon of pepper. Simmer a moment or two and serve.

2. Heat one can of white sauce and two cups of milk. When smooth, add eight ounces of clams, including the juice. Let the mixture come to a boil. Season with the same amount of salt and pepper as used in the first recipe, simmer it, and serve. Both recipes serve four.

Veal Chop with Paprika and Egg Noodles

Put one-half cup milk and a can of white sauce in a saucepan with two teaspoonfuls of paprika; bring the mixture to a boil, and beat with an egg beater or whisk. Now take four veal chops, which you have previously browned and cooked in a skillet for thirty-five to forty-five minutes, remove from the skillet and set aside. Add about one-half cup of water to the skillet, cook for two minutes, and add this to the sauce, mixing it with an egg beater. Cover the chops with the sauce and serve with noodles boiled to taste. Serves four.

Cheese Soufflé

Many people have trouble making soufflés; this one can be mastered instantly by a child. Heat one can of white sauce. Beat and mix in one-half cup grated Parmesan cheese and three egg yolks. Let the mixture cool. Put it in four individual casseroles and bake for ten minutes at 325° and then for fifteen at 350°. Serves four.

Creamed Oysters

To one pint raw oysters add one-half pint cold water, put in a saucepan, let the mixture come to a boil and simmer until the oysters curl up lightly. Bring to a boil in another pan one can of white sauce to which you have added one-half cup milk and an equal portion of oyster liquor, drained from the cooked oysters. Smooth this mixture with an egg beater. Add the oysters and liquid and heat all together. Season with one-half teaspoon of salt, one-quarter teaspoon of paprika or pepper, and a dash of Lea and Perrins sauce if you desire. Serve on toast or with boiled potatoes. Serves four or five.

Curry of Lamb

Get about one and one-half pounds of boned lamb shoulder or neck and cut it in one-inch cubes. Brown it lightly in a skillet. Add three teaspoons of curry powder and one of salt, simmer for a minute, add one-half cup water, one-quarter cup tomato juice, and the same amount of apple juice. Cover the skillet and cook over a low fire until tender, which would be anywhere from one hour to one and one-half. Now, in a saucepan, mix one can of white sauce and one-half cup milk, bring to a boil, and smooth with an egg beater. Add this to the meat when it is finished cooking, stir together, let it come to a boil once more, and serve. This should take care of from six to eight people.

Eggs with Spinach Florentine

Bring to a boil one can of white sauce to which has been added one cup of milk, two tablespoons of grated Parmesan cheese, one teaspoonful of salt, and several pinches of pepper. Smooth it with an egg beater. Add six sliced hard-cooked eggs. Let the mixture come to a boil. In a buttered baking dish put one and one-half cups cooked tender spinach. Pour in the mixture with the eggs and spread it around. Sprinkle grated Parmesan cheese on top, pour on some melted butter, and brown under the broiler. This will serve four to six people nicely.

Rock Lobster À La Tosca

To one can of white sauce add one small can of evaporated milk and one-half can of lobster liquid or water. Bring the

ingredients to a boil and smooth with an egg beater. Add two
five and one-half ounce cans of rock lobster or the equivalent
of fresh or frozen lobster. Simmer for five minutes. Stir occasionally. Before serving, add one teaspoonful paprika and
two good dashes of sherry wine. Serves four.

Veal Fricassee with Vegetables

For this, get about three pounds of boneless shoulder of
veal and cut it in two-inch squares. (Breast of veal will also
do.) Wash the meat and put it in a saucepan with enough
hot water to cover it. Season with two teaspoons of salt and
one-half teaspoon of pepper. Bring to a boil and simmer for
anywhere from one and one-half to two hours, or until tender. Now bring to a boil one can of white sauce to which has
been added one-half cup of milk and an equal portion of the
veal broth. Smooth it with an egg beater. Drain the meat.
Add it to the sauce, along with one-half cup each of diced
carrots, cooked peas, and cooked small onions. Toss in one
teaspoonful of chopped parsley. Let everything come to a
boil for two minutes. Serve this with noodles, boiled potatoes,
or rice. It feeds four or five.

Boiled Salmon Steak with Sauce Allemande

Boil one and one-half pounds of salmon steaks in four cups
of water with two teaspoons of salt and two tablespoons of
vinegar. Bring to a boil one can of white sauce with one-half
cup each of milk and salmon liquid and the juice of one
lemon. Smooth the sauce with an egg beater, simmer one
minute, and just before serving over the salmon, add two egg
yolks and mix well. This serves four to six.

Chicken Tetrazzini

Boil about four ounces of spaghetti to taste and drain it.
Set aside in a colander. To one can of white sauce add three-
quarters of a cup of milk, bring it to a boil, and smooth with
an egg beater. Add one cup of cooked diced chicken, four

tablespoons of grated Parmesan cheese, and a three-ounce can of chopped mushrooms and their liquid. Mix the ingredients well. Put the spaghetti in a buttered baking dish. Pour over the sauce. Shred over it more Parmesan cheese and dot with lumps of butter. Brown under the broiler. Serves four.

CHAPTER FIFTEEN

A Postscript

IT MAY ONLY BE MY IMAGINATION, but it sometimes occurs to me that there are certain things which do not change —and certain people. These days when I walk through Sardi's, I sometimes have to reassure myself that I am in the present and not living ten, fifteen, or twenty years ago. For one thing, certain faces always seem to remain the same—and some of them, I swear it, look better than ever. My wife and I saw Vivienne Segal soon after she came out of retirement in 1952 to appear in the revival of *Pal Joey*, and we exclaimed to each other over her youthful appearance; she actually looked younger, to me, than she did when she appeared in the same part back in the thirties. Fifteen years ago, at least, we gave a party for Maurice Evans in our place —I remember it particularly, because my old friend Don Freeman did a life-size portrait of him that was the center of attention; and yet, when Evans opened in *Dial M for Murder* last year, he looked no older. When I saw Robert Montgomery on television one night recently, he was the same young man who used to come into Sardi's in the old days. There is something very reassuring about the ability these people have to remain young. The only time I become conscious of change is when I look about the restaurant and expect to see Winthrop Ames or Kelcey Allen or Bide Dudley or any of the regular patrons. My eyes, I confess, get a little wet when I think that I have not seen them for some time and will not see them again. Then I think of others who have gone—of Frederick Arnold Kummer, the writer, who in addition to turning out many things of his own also collaborated with Victor Herbert and Sigmund Romberg; of Robert Loraine, who appeared in *The Master of the Inn*, one of the shows in which our Cino had a part; of Irvin S. Cobb, who always had people smiling with his dry humor; of Richard Washburn Child, the lawyer and novelist who later became ambassador to Italy; of Frazer Coulter, the character actor, who died at eighty-eight, wishing he could return to the stage in a wheelchair; and of the jolly Ted Healy, who died in Hollywood shortly after his wife had given birth to a son.

Yes, I must admit that I long for the days when those people were around; but I console myself by remembering that they all led good, full lives, and that they all provided amusement for many people. When Jenny and I go to the theater these days and stop in at Sardi's afterward, I get to feeling even better, for now the place is full of young actors and actresses, all busy at their work, all trying to make names for themselves, just as the youngsters did when I was active.

Some of them I recognize, and some I don't. Some I remember coming in with their parents, and some I remember coming in at such an early age that I was almost prompted to tell them to go home and wait until they were old enough to come in by themselves, without older people to make them mind their manners. Several have already established their names; Geraldine Page, who was acclaimed a star in *Midsummer* last year; Daniel Mann, who directed Shirley Booth in both the stage and movie versions of *Come Back, Little Sheba;* Charlton Heston and Marlon Brando, who are both doing well in the movies; Michael Sloane, producer of *Top*

Banana with his wife, Paula Stone; Ronny Graham, Eartha Kitt, and Alice Ghostley, who were in the most recent *New Faces;* Arthur Kennedy and Alfred Drake, good friends of Cino, both of whom have done so much they are by now regarded as seasoned, well-established stars. And there are others, all active in the theater, whose names mean something to the public: Betsy von Furstenberg, Kevin McCarthy, Robert Quarry, Pat Englund, Cloris Leachman, Ralph Meeker, Meg Mundy, Geraldine Brooks and her sister Gloria, Barbara Bel Geddes, Beverly Bozeman, Bob Shearer, Lydia Clarke, Diana Lynn, Margaret Philipps, Constance Dowling . . .

They all come, these youngsters and many others, and the fact that they do come is what makes me feel so good. It makes my life have a second meaning; it means that I did more than start a restaurant which is being carried on by my son. It means that Sardi's is actually a part of the theater, and will continue to be a part for some time to come. Even more, it means to me that opportunity in this country is still alive for everyone. It was there for an immigrant boy, and it is still here, nearly a half century afterward, for these young people. There is nothing they cannot do, in the theater or in any other business, as long as they work hard and live according to principle. That is what Sardi's means to me. I hope it will go on meaning the same thing.

Index